Table of Contents

Dedication 7

Acknowledgements 9

Staff 11

Coasters 13

Introduction 15

Preparation 19

Prologue 21

California 23

Arizona 37

New Mexico 81

Texas 93

Louisiana 173

Mississippi 193

Alabama 201

Florida 211

Dedication

Coast to Coast with Bubba's Pampered Pedalers is dedicated to the wonderful work Jeff and Lisa Arndt are doing through their support of Custom Canines Service Dog Academy. The Arndt's raise funds for this non-profit academy tasked with selecting, training, and providing specialty dogs to act as companions and helpmates for people suffering from autism and PTSD. They were riding the C2C as a fundraiser for this important cause and offered speciality jerseys to aid their fundraising efforts.

The puzzle pieces on the jersey signify the difficulty people with autism and PTSD have integrating the pieces of their lives into a cohesive picture. The dogs sense this tendency to disorientation and help steer those afflicted away from making poor choices as they venture forth into the world.

All profits from the sale of this book will be donated to Custom Canines Service Dog Academy. Thank you for your support.

Acknowledgements

Thanks to Bubba and all the wonderful staff members who made this trip a memorable treasure. Their effort lived up to every possible definition of pampering one could imagine.

Thanks to Wayne Andresen, John Holden, and Jeff and Lisa Arndt for allowing me to reference their blogs, paraphrase their insights, and use photos they took along the route. Thanks too to Greg Townley and Cecil Goettsch for their photos of the Coasters and the staff.

Thanks to Coaster Joe Nelson for his poem on Aging Well found at the end of the book.

Special thanks to my brother-in-law Tom Foor and his sister Linda without whose encouragement I never would have attempted this adventure.

Universal thanks to all forty-four participating cyclists who enabled us to come together as a community of individuals concerned for each other's welfare as we struggled with the difficulties and celebrated with the successes we encountered along our amazing bicycle ride across America.

I'll be forever in debt to Ms. Taryn Heon for her editorial insights and proofreading skills for without them it would have been obvious this book was written by an engineer.

Final thanks to Google for providing maps included in this book.

Sam Hawkes
August 2015

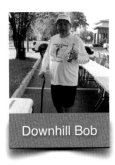

Downhill Bob

Gary

Greg

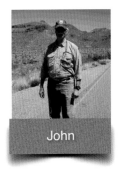

John

Chandler

Bubba's Pampered Pedalers
2015
Coast to Coast
Staff

Hans

Joyce & Ed

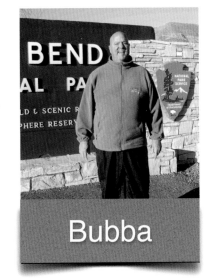

Bubba

Marge

Rose & John

Serge & Anne

Snowflake

Cocoa Bean

Aaron & Craig

The Wolfpack
Adam, Peach Fuzz,
Chester, Cyrano & Zach

Alan

Barb

Beth

Don

Bruce

Bubba's Pampered Pedalers
2015
Coasters

Dan

Cecil

Dave

Loren

Eddy

Frances

Monica

Greg

Gordon

Dean

Randy

Colleen

Jeff

Lisa

Coach

Joe

Bob

Graham

Ken-1

Ken-2

Gail

Marla

 Judy

 Jim

 Larry

 John

 Woody

 Tom

 Linda

 Sam

 Ron

 Nancy

 Udi

 Rich

 Mike

 Marianne

 Phil

 Wayne

 Roger

Introduction

Many cyclists cross the country each year. Some go by themselves charting their own routes and carrying all the gear necessary for roadside camping. Most, however, sign up with an organized tour group so all they have to worry about is riding their bicycles. The group handles lodging, meals, luggage transportation, and emergency services. This book is a documentation of just such a group trip by one such cyclist, a senior cyclist, who went with a tour conducted by Bubba's Pampered Pedalers.

We started in San Diego, California and finished in St. Augustine, Florida, a total distance of 2909 miles, not counting side trips. It took a total of fifty-two days, forty-four of which were devoted to cycling. We rested for eight of those fifty-two days. Bubba's Pampered Pedalers provided total support services, from transporting our luggage to setting up campsites and feeding us two meals a day. We were pampered to be sure, but then we weren't spring chickens, and most of us had done our Boy Scout/Girl Scout time as adolescents; the excitement of setting up a tent and cooking over an open fire having dimmed. We were a group of forty-four, thirteen women and thirty-one men, whose average age was sixty-three. Our oldest was a lady of seventy-five and youngest a lady of fifty. A few were very strong riders, but most of us took our time pumping out the daily miles, swallowing Advil, and sleeping long hours to restore our strength. Of the forty-four who started the tour, forty finished. One had a spill and broke his arm, another suffered an eye condition and was advised to discontinue, and two had to return home for personal reasons. One of our members had a heart attack, but returned to the tour in two weeks after receiving a stent. Cyclists are a stout bunch!

I wouldn't have attempted such an adventure without Tom's encouragement. Tom, my brother-in-law had been an avid cyclist all his life and we were good friends when he married my sister. I owned a bicycle, but I didn't ride to the extent Tom rode, and I didn't learn until later that he had ambitions to race professionally. When I retired, Tom convinced me that I should take up cycling seriously not only for my health, but so he would have a companion with whom to ride. With this in mind I bought a twenty-four speed Trek Pilot and began working out. Together we took several supported tours, one across Georgia, one across Utah, and another through the Canadian Rockies. We were joined by Tom's sister, Linda, and the three of us made a fun family unit during these junkets.

During our Bike Ride Across Georgia (BRAG) the three of us signed up to use a tent service operated by Bubba Barron, and he introduced us to the idea of riding across the country. I laughed at the idea and immediately put it out of my mind, but it found traction with Tom, and it wasn't long before Tom began making noises about how we ought to look into it. This wasn't too surprising since he was the one who at one time wanted to be a professional cyclist. I'd never had any such compunction, and when he first suggested we should explore the possibilities, I was incredulous. Why, I thought, would I ever want to do something like that? All of my friends were playing golf and growing tomatoes, comfortable in their retirements having earned the right to take it easy until the end. So when Tom first suggested it, I strongly and vociferously registered a negative response. And yet, the seed was planted. About three months after he suggested we go, I relented as did his sister Linda. As it was, it turned out to be one of the signature events of my life.

After I agreed to join Tom and Linda on this sea-to-sea journey with Bubba, I was stuck with the question of why I had signed up to do it in the first place. When I told others I had planned to ride my bike across America, their eyes would squint, deep lines would appear across their foreheads, and through anguished, painful facial expressions they would form the words, "Why would anyone want to do that?"

Why, indeed? It's the question I kept asking myself over and over ever since Tom suggested we do it. I could hardly get through a one-day, sixty-mile ride, and the Prouty Century (100-mile) Ride I went on to benefit the Dartmouth-Hitchcock Norris Cotton Cancer Center in 2014 wiped me out for a week. I had to admit, I was awfully proud of the century ride and could only imagine how proud I'd be if I were to string a couple of months of such days together. Certainly I was influenced by the movie, *The Bucket List*, in which two senior citizens make a list of all the things they want to do before they kick the bucket. I knew I'd be proud to say I rode my bike across America as relatives gathered at my bedside to bid me farewell. I liked to imagine them shaking their heads in disbelief, "You know, this old fossil rode his bicycle across America when he was seventy-two! What a guy."

Besides the pride of accomplishment, Tom is one of my closest friends, and I looked forward to spending as much time with him as possible. This was not an easy task as I lived in New Hampshire and he lived in California. We visited when we could, but as our friends and relatives became indisposed, we both realized that time was running out.

Another factor that entered the equation was Bubba's organizational ability. Bubba provided great service during the BRAG ride setting up tents, blowing up air mattresses, and providing a congenial ambiance at the end of a hard riding day. With Bubba orchestrating two meals a day, all we would have to do is ride our bikes from campground to campground, or in a few instances, from campground to motel, and forget about everything else. It would be a two month vacation, albeit a working one, with all the amenities of a Caribbean Cruise.

And then it had to be, in part, the allure of having a straightforward, attainable goal to which I could spend six months preparing, and one that I'd have a good shot at completing successfully.

So I said, "OK, Tom let's do it!"

However, before Bubba would accept anyone on his tour, we had to call him and explain our situation.

"Listen," he said, "the worst thing that can happen on a tour like this is to have even one person who is a whiner. Whiners spread a poison among the group either garnering sympathy for their misery or support for their complaints. This tour is an adventure, not a cake walk. You will be tired, hungry, thirsty, hot, cold, sweaty, achy, and challenged every day. If you decide you want to come along, I want no complaints. Agreed?"

"Uhhhhh. . . Agreed," I managed to eke out from a constricted throat, wondering what I had gotten myself in for.

But I did it, and this book is about my sea-to-sea - C2C- adventure. It contains some thoughts about preparing for such an effort, but mainly it is a tale of discovery as I traversed the southern tier of the United States on my bicycle. Perhaps if you've considered going on such an adventure but hesitated out of fear for the unknown, you'll glean some insights from my experience. Hesitate no longer. You will have the time of your life!

California, Arizona, New Mexico, Texas, Louisiana, Mississippi, Alabama, Florida

Preparation

Never having done anything before quite the magnitude of a two month, three-thousand -mile bicycle trip, I knew I needed to get my body in better shape. My first thought was to lose some weight, so I set a goal to lose twenty pounds by March 7, the date we were scheduled to leave San Diego. I was hitting the scales at one-ninety, and losing twenty pounds would put me in an ideal weight for my advanced age. I knew too, that carrying an extra twenty pound bag of lard strapped to my midriff was going to make any hill I had to climb that much harder. To lose the weight, I gave myself a three-month regimen of exercise and diet in the artisanal city of Oaxaca, Mexico where I stayed at Linda's B & B. Since she was doing the C2C as well as I, it seemed we could support each other in sticking to whatever regimen we chose.

In Oaxaca I rode a hybrid bike ten miles to and from the Calypso Fitness Center where Linda and I worked out daily for two hours under our trainer's watchful eye. We'd spend the first half hour on treadmills or elliptical cyclers to get our heart rates up and sweat glands open. We'd then shift to the muscle building machines where we'd work for an hour either on our lower bodies or on our upper bodies, alternating between the two every other day. After doing four repetitions on each of ten machines, we'd finish off the session with half an hour either on an Exercycle or a stair-stepper. Linda elected to do the routine without the bike ride to-and-from Calypso, leading me to believe I was bound to be in better shape than she at the start of the tour. Silly me to be so presumptive.

Following my stay south of the border, I returned to my home in Keene, NH and spent the next two months working out at the YMCA. Keene has a fabulous new facility where I was able to swim for half an hour to get my heart rate up, run on a treadmill for half an hour to build my lung capacity, and then engage in spin classes for my cycling muscles. The spin classes turned out to be one of the most difficult exercise regimens in which I have ever engaged. There were about twenty stationary bikes in the spin room, and, in addition to the bikes, there were two massive speakers for pounding out heavy metal rock in time with your pedaling speed. A facilitator issued instructions for resistance settings (hills), "OK, turn the knob three turns. I want you to feel your muscles burn." and cadence (speed), "Now, back off the knob two turns and give me all you have. Give me more. More, MORE!" All this will be going on while music is being played at volumes approaching the threshold of pain. Maybe the decibels hammering your brain through your eardrums are supposed to drown out the screams emanating from your overworked muscles. Whatever their intent, the end of all my spin classes were anticipated with a huge sense of welcome relief. I can't say for sure if the spin classes I had attended helped get me ready for the trek, but they couldn't have hurt, as I felt fit and well prepared when the day came for us to head out from San Diego.

As far as diet was concerned, I didn't pay much attention to special foods. I knew exercise burned protein, so having plenty of protein to supplement an exercise routine was high on my list of priorities. I managed to lose fifteen pounds toward my goal of twenty the three months I was in Mexico by simply focusing on fruits and proteins and staying away from bread, rice, potatoes and pasta. I heard that Sofia Loren once said, "Everything you see I owe to spaghetti." My response at the time was, "Yeah man, viva spaghetti," but, when she made that comment, much of what you saw was between her knees and her navel so I knew pasta would be counterproductive to my mission. Natural fats are welcomed by the body, and fortunately avocados are plentiful in Mexico. I ate guacamole on a daily basis. I can't say I really paid much attention to eating any less for the three months I was in Mexico, but cutting whites and fermented grapes out of my diet seemed to do the trick.

We were advised by the mechanic assigned to our passage to have our bicycles serviced prior to the ride. This service included checking and replacing cables, checking chains and sprockets for signs of wear, and buying new tires. He also let us know that we should be prepared for problems en route and advised we stock up on tubes (at least four), Continental Gatorskin tires (two), replacement chain, and spare spokes. We all needed to carry a kit on our bicycles to include enough tools to repair a flat and fix a broken chain. We would have a flat tire, we might even have many, many flat tires, so we needed to learn how to replace or repair our tubes.

The seat, ahhh, the seat. Our nether regions were going to take quite a beating, so we were advised to outfit our bikes with a seat on which we had done a lot of riding and on which we felt most comfortable. As a precaution, I took an extra seat along just in case my favorite seat started causing me undue distress. I wanted to give my crotch the relief of different pressure points by the use of a different seat, if even for a day or two. Of all the physical agonies endured on the tour, my crotch suffered the most. I think after a while the nerves in one's crotch just give up. I know mine did, and the final month in the saddle caused me little discomfort.

In researching different ways to prepare for long distance cycle trips, there was one that made the most sense but was the least help: "The best way to train for a 3000-mile bike ride is to ride your bike for 3000 miles." In the ten years I'd been riding I don't think I'd ridden a total of 3000 miles. I was about to find out if I could do it in six weeks.

Prologue

Honda CRV Ready to GO!

Toward the end of February, Linda flew up to California from Mexico - I flew out to California from New Hampshire. We met at Tom's place in the San Francisco Bay Area from where we planned some shake down bike trips in the Napa and Sonoma Valleys. On March 5th we headed south to San Diego with three bikes clamped on the top of Tom's Honda and every available cubic inch of interior space consumed with people or pack sacks.

The next day, we arrived at the Ocean Beach Motel in San Diego where we would start our journey. We made it to San Diego a day early, and once we had unpacked the CRV, we drove it empty east of San Diego to Jamul to leave it with Tom's cousin Tim. Tim had agreed to garage the car for the two months we'd be on the road to the East Coast. Tim is a whirlwind of a fellow and spends his time building hot rods and making model train layouts. We enjoyed a delightful dinner with him and his lovely wife, Norma, before he chauffeured the three of us back to the Ocean Beach Motel.

The following morning was free, so Linda and I biked out to the National Park at Point Loma. In the afternoon, we all assembled to attend the kickoff party Bubba had arranged for us Coasters. At the party, we each took a minute, some more minutes than others, to introduce ourselves and explain to the best of our abilities why we were making this trek across the country.

Tim Foor With His Hot Rod

I was nervous, not scared really, but a bit trepidatious. I wanted so much to succeed in making it across the country, but I had no idea whether I would be able to do it. Would I be strong enough? Would my heart give out? Would I cramp up so badly I couldn't go on? Would I suffer a hideous accident, maybe even die en route? I had a lot on my mind as I drifted off to sleep that last night in San Diego.

March 7 - Day 1

San Diego to Alpine
42 miles

Map data ©2015 Google

The day broke clear and calm over Ocean Beach in San Diego. There was an electric anticipation in the air as all the riders emerged from their rooms at the Ocean Villa Hotel and convened in the breakfast area. Most everyone was up early, and the dining room was filled at six-thirty am - a completely unnecessary early rising as we weren't scheduled to do our "Wheel Dipping" until nine. Bubba had several tables set up in the parking lot on which he had laid out all the articles of clothing to be issued to the participants. First was our fluorescent yellow safety vest on which one of the staff carefully printed everyone's first name. We were strongly advised to wear the vest at all times so we'd be visible to motorists, and the names helped us all to remember the names of those we had just met. This was a nice touch as we seniors are legend for forever forgetting names.

Safety Vest

C2C Jersey Front

We then picked up our Coast-to-Coast cycling jerseys with a picture of the pier at San Diego on the front and a picture of a Saguaro cactus on the back. Each of us then received a yellow t-shirt and yellow long-sleeved shirt with the names of every town where we would be spending the

C2C Jersey Back

night printed on the front. Afterwards we received a fleece jacket, a long-sleeved grey shirt, and a promise of a Bubba Beanie which was still on a ship moored off Long Beach thanks to a longshoreman's strike on the west coast. A final contribution from Bubba was a yellow rain slicker, a rather sober reminder that this journey was going to be an adventure and not a cake walk. In addition to fending off rain, the slicker would serve us well as a handy wind breaker for those cooler mornings. Eventually we all took to carrying it with us stuck in our jersey pockets, stuffed into a saddle bag, or tied to our seats with bungie cords.

Before leaving for the beach we celebrated the six nations represented on the tour: the USA, Canada, Mexico, Germany, Holland, and the UK. Once picture taking at the motel came to a close, we were off. We walked down to the beach, all forty-four of us, carrying our bikes so that sand wouldn't get into the gears, and then we formed a single line in front of the ocean. After the photo shoot, which lasted until the incoming tide had soaked everyone's feet, we headed out for Alpine.

USA, Canada, Mexico, Germany, Holland, England

Truth be told my nerves were still on edge. I kept thinking about Bubba describing the trip as an adventure with what seemed a myriad of elements that would make it miserable. Would my body give out on a cold ascent? Would a speeding semi-

Wheel Dipping in the Pacific Ocean

trailer blow me off the road? Would I take a wrong turn and get lost in the desert? Certainly adventures are comprised of just such uncertainties, otherwise they wouldn't be adventures, but I had never done anything like this in my life, and I felt the same sense of anxiety I used to feel before I played a high-school football game. I learned later that many on the tour were just as nervous as I.

The day was glorious with cloudless skies, little wind, and temperatures in the 80s. The route was complicated with many different roads taking us in a generally eastern direction, but they were well marked with arrows laid down by Bubba's support team. This part of California is very bicycle friendly, and there were bike lanes on all the roads we traversed. The only close call I witnessed, and it didn't even involve a bicycle, was a near T-bone at a high-speed intersection when a car pulled out in front of a pickup which peeled off the road and went through a picket fence. The driver was shaken but unhurt and the car that pulled out sped off. I always think at these times that I'll be aware enough to get a license number, but of course I never do.

Our route took us through Friar Junipero Serra County Park, the unincorporated area of Alpine, and the Viejas Reservation of the Kumeyaay tribe of Native Americans. Viejas comes from the Spanish who originally named the area, "Valle de las Viejas" translated into English as Valley of the Old Ladies. I breezed through Alpine without really knowing it was there, but as soon as I entered the Viejas Reservation I was welcomed by a casino, an outlet store, and a bowling alley. Our first night was spent at the Ma Tar Awa Viejas Camper Park, located roughly two miles east of Alpine and within the Viejas Reservation. The park was a lovely setting with scrub oaks and chaparral populating the rolling landscape. The day's trek required some of the group to climb more hills on their bikes than they had ever done prior to, so our group filtered into the park throughout the afternoon. I was feeling more refreshed than tired, a very good sign, but I suspected it was due more to the endorphin load in my system than any sign that I was in good physical shape. My nerves had completely calmed down upon arrival into the campsite.

When we arrived at the campground, our tents were set up, our air mattresses inflated, and our luggage placed inside our tents waiting for us. Bubba provided a central gathering spot with phone charging stations, bins of various snacks, and coolers of beverages. You can see our spot under the blue pop-ups in the background. The snacks and soft drinks were free, but the alcoholic beverages required a donation in the form of a token the riders purchased

Bubba Domes with Common Area in Background

from our drinks coordinator, Downhill Bob. Throughout the trek, I never found out how Bob earned the moniker "Downhill," but I liked to imagine him tearing down a well-paved, outrageously steep hill, pedaling madly and screaming "Geronimo" at the top of

Gourmet Buffet Every Night!

his lungs. After our adventure, Bob let on that a riding companion had called him "Downhill Bob" because he always told her it was, "all downhill from here." Bob was a warm and accommodating friend to all of us, especially those who chose to imbibe. He went out of his way to make sure he had a good stock of all the specialty drinks anyone wanted. My favorite was the Starbucks Mocha, probably because my body was lusting for sugar. And, boy, is the Starbucks Mocha loaded with sugar. Another favorite for some of us was chocolate milk that we downed by the quart every chance we got.

At around six-o'clock every night Anne and Serge served up dinner prepared from their mobile kitchen called The Culinary Insider. These two amazing people bought all the food for both breakfast and dinner, and then prepared what can only be described as gourmet feasts for the forty-four riders and eighteen support staff. Even though Anne was trained as a chef, it seemed somewhat miraculous to me that so much great food could come from one small, mobile kitchen staffed by only one cook and one helper. That first night in Alpine we were treated to ribeye roast, rosemary chicken, baked potatoes, curried vegetables, tossed salad, and banana cream pie. One thing about cycling for long distances, your body burns a large number of calories, some say sixty calories per mile, so none of us had any compunction about eating our fill of everything. Anne knew from past experience that cyclists tended to keep coming back to the trough, and she always prepared enough for everyone to have seconds. My hat is really off to these two!

And then, after dinner, I headed straight for my tent and was sawing zees the second I hit my mattress.

March 8 - Day 2

Alpine to Live Oak Springs
32 Miles

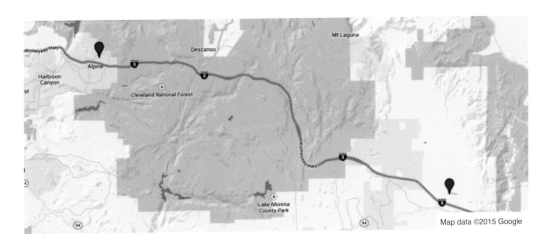

The night in Alpine started off mild, but as the evening wore on the temperature dropped and by morning it was in the high thirties. The nighttime cold was due to the clear desert air which allows heat generated during the day to escape rapidly into space at night. I arose shivering in the morning and headed immediately for a sunny spot to absorb what heat I could from the rising sun. It didn't rise as early as it was supposed to thanks to the mountains so the cold stayed around quite a while. One enterprising cyclist started a fire in a campfire pit to which as many as could elbow their way in gathered around. The air did warm up rather rapidly as soon as the sun emerged and we all basked in it to thwart the chill. Check out Jeff on the stump.

Jeff Journaling in the Sun

March 8th being a Sunday, the tour held a brief interdenominational service in the morning conducted by Ed Gillette, one of our volunteer staff members. Ed played a major role in conducting services for his church at home, so his talents were put to good use in organizing music, prayers, and positive thoughts for the day. Ed and I had some interesting discussions on religion later in the tour, and I developed a deep respect for his faith. I didn't subscribe to the letter of his beliefs, but we found a lot of common ground on such topics as original sin and eternal life.

The hours in the gym really paid off today as it was a day of climbing and climbing and climbing to an elevation of 4000 feet. I was far from the first to leave the campground but came in at the front of the pack in Live Oak Springs. This wasn't necessarily because I was faster than anyone else, but only that others stopped more often to take pictures and rest at the SAG stops. We passed through a quaint village called Pine Valley where I stopped at a statue in someone's front yard made completely of the plastic containers used to grow plants for sale at your local nursery. This person painted all hers yellow and then made a yellow flower pot Michelin woman with a bouquet for a hat. It was pure whimsy, and I was enchanted enough to stop and snap a photo. There were many such displays of artistic expression along our cross country route, and I was forever impressed with the extent to which people will go to for the amusement of those traveling through.

Flower Pot Lady

Live Oak Springs Market

It took roughly three hours to go the thirty-two miles, which wasn't too bad considering there was so much uphill. Our destination was the Live Oak Springs Market, which was just about all that there seemed to be in Live Oak Springs. The market carried all the essentials for daily survival: gas, food, and liquor.

The nighttime temperatures at this 4000 ft. elevation drop well below the temperatures in Alpine 2000 feet lower. Last year the tour stayed in Live Oak Springs, and water bottles left outside the tents froze solid. We learned that riders inside the tents froze solid too, but adhering to the "no whine" mandate handed down by Bubba at the onset, everybody emerged from their sleeping bags remarking how "refreshing" the evening air had become. The potential for frozen Coasters was such that Bubba decided we should all leave our bikes there in Live Oak Springs and return to Ma Tak Awa by shuttle to spend the night at a lower elevation where it wouldn't be so cold.

We left our bikes in a sheep pen to the side of the market that had been converted to a storage yard just for us. Once sufficient riders had arrived at the market site to fill a van, we were driven the thirty-two miles back to Ma Tak Awa. Linda, Dan, and I then collapsed in the campground hot tub to soak our aching muscles. Recognize that thirty-two miles really isn't very far for an avid road cyclist, but we were climbing the whole way, many of us for the first time at such a distance, and the hot water felt great as it swirled around our legs. Bubba confided in us later that he worried all night about the security of the sheep pen. There really was nothing to prevent an enterprising thief to drive off with a couple hundred thousand dollars worth of bicycles in the middle of the night.

Now, as far as the SAG stop referred to above, officially I think SAG means Support, Assistance, and Gear, though I've heard it means Support And Gear, and also Stop And Go. All meanings are correct in their interpretation. A SAG stop is a place set up by tour organizers where weary cyclists can get moral Support, receive Assistance in the form of drinks and snacks, and get help with Gear in need of repair. Bubba organized SAG stops about every twenty to thirty miles with bins of iced down soft drinks, coolers of water and powdered G2, candy bars, power bars, crackers, cookies, fresh fruit, potato chips, peanut butter

Typical SAG Stop

and... you get the picture. Bubba was religious about sanitation, and it was mandatory that we all used hand sanitizer before touching any food at a SAG stop. Past tours have had trouble with intestinal infestations among the riders, and, thanks to all the sanitizing, there was no sign of any such problem during the 2015 C2C.

SAG stops also allow a cyclist to shed any unwanted clothing that might have been needed in the cool of the morning but was not needed as the sun came up. This clothing was then required to be picked up from the bins at the end of the day. Clothing that wasn't picked up was then presented at dinner with appropriate hoots from the audience as the forgetful owner stepped forward. Incredible as it may seem, the clothing bin began to accumulate leftovers, as cyclists either couldn't identify their own clothing or didn't want to face the embarrassment of having forgotten to pick it up. By the time we arrived in St. Augustine the clothing bin was half full.

March 9 - Day 3

Live Oak Springs to Calexico
63 Miles

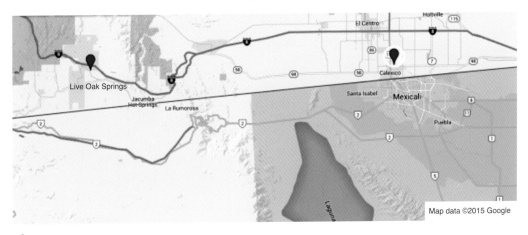

The day dawned early back in the Alpine camp (Daylight Savings) and was stinging cold for all of us who didn't bring much to wear. Breakfast consisted of tortilla wrapped bacon and eggs and generous cups of coffee. Since the bikes were all stacked in the sheep pen in Live Oak Springs, and, because mine was in first, it made no sense for me to get to the Live Oak Springs Market ahead of anyone else; I wasn't going anywhere until everyone had hit the road anyway. As a result, I was bussed to Live Oak Springs last, which in fact was a good deal; by the time I recovered my bike the day was rapidly warming up. I don't like to bike in the cold.

Canal from the Colorado River

The first ten miles out from Live Oak Springs consisted of long downhill stretches over smooth pavement as we descended 4000 feet into the Imperial Valley. The Valley contains some of the best farm lands in the country due to overflows from the Colorado River which, in prior years, used to flood the land with rich topsoil before it was controlled by upstream dams. As a result of the rich farmland, and near perfect hot, cloudless days, agriculture forms the basis for the region's economy, generating a billion dollars worth of income to the region each year. Colorado river water is distributed to the farmlands through canals and underground aqueducts, and it fuels an agricultural juggernaut limited only by its availability. The volume is often determined by the snow pack in the Rocky Mountains, but rarely is any but a trickle left in the river by the time it reaches the Gulf of California. Mexico isn't too happy about that.

Solar Energy Panels

Because of the abundance of sun in the valley, it is also a perfect location for solar energy. We saw miles and miles of solar panels as we crossed the less fertile sections of the valley, and these, with accompanying wind farms, provided many kilowatts of electrical power to the region. It's been said the power from such installations isn't competitive with conventional power sources from petroleum products, but the hope is in time the costs will come down as producers of solar panels learn how to make them economically.

Wind Turbine Farm

The Valley is noted for its sun and its heat, but also for many other things. Cher, of the singing duo Sonny and Cher, was born in Calexico, our destination for the night, as was Tokyo Rose, the lady behind the sexy voice luring our soldiers to their ruin during WWII. Also, the San Andreas fault that most of us associate with San Francisco runs right through Calexico, and in 2010 an earthquake killed four people, injured one hundred, and leveled many houses in the city. These were historical tidbits I knew nothing about before embarking on this journey.

As we hit the valley, temperatures rose into the high 80s. Mile after mile we cycled along more or less straight, undulating road with the heat little by little taking its toll on me and I assumed others as well. I downed great draughts of Gatorade and filled up my empty bottles at the SAG stops. Aside from the heat, one drawback about cycling in the Valley is the straight road. There is something discouraging about biking down long, straight roads disappearing to a vanishing point ten miles distant. The effort to get to

that vanishing point seems excessive and often when one arrives there, particularly in the Southwest, all that can be seen is another vanishing point ten miles distant. Such was the case crossing the Imperial Valley to Calexico. It was our longest day yet and our hottest day yet, with little to see but vast acres of desert, alfalfa fields, solar panels and wind farms.

Long, Straight Roads Vanishing in the Distance

Now, you will note a black line crossing the picture of the long, straight road through the valley. This is America's border fence with Mexico, a rather sad commentary on our country's inability to deal with the immigrant situation between us and our neighbors to the south. It reminded me too much of the reviled Berlin Wall to make me feel comfortable with it. Along our route we passed border patrol stations and parking lots full of new Border Patrol SUVs all gassed up and ready to chase down the "criminals". I understood drones might be used for patrolling the fence, but I didn't see any in operation that day. However I did see a couple of gliders

Immigration Department Gliders?

stationed along the fence (black line behind the gliders) and assumed they were used for other than recreational purposes. Our trek took us for miles along the border, so we had many opportunities to witness the country's efforts to keep people out.

Little by little, we Coasters all drifted into Calexico, a city of 40,000 that started as a tent city back in 1899 housing workers for the Imperial Land Company. The Company was established to convert the desert into agricultural plantations, which it did with great success. Back when the city was founded, the border was porous and the tent city expanded to cover both sides of the boundary between the USA and Mexico. When it came time to incorporate the cities, they were given names to cement their common history but distinguish their different allegiances - Calexico on the USA side and Mexicali on the Mexican side. The current population of Mexicali is close to 700,000; it is the capital of Baja California and an industrial center fueled by maquiladora manufacturing operations in Free Trade Zones established by the Mexican government. If the tent city was once situated on an amorphous border, today that same border is defined by our tall fence running right down the center of the two cities and right next to the Calexico Mission School where we were spending the night.

Our Stop for the Night

Dinner at the Mission School

By dinner time we had all arrived at the mission school run by Seventh Day Adventists. It catered only to Spanish speaking children from Mexico. They all had visas, and they all crossed the border each day from their homes in Mexicali to get to the school. Dinner was served to us by the students at the Mission School and was followed by a discussion about the school by the Headmistress Susan Smith, a Canadian who has been with the school for twenty-four years. She was exuded a charming aura as she explained the founding of the school and its mission to bring a message of tolerance and understanding all who attended. The students who waited on us serving dinner were as polite as could be and all spoke excellent English. Bubba took great pleasure in introducing each student and asking them a bit about their background.

Bubba also encouraged anyone in the group to speak up after dinner if they had anything they wished to share with the group, and my brain wouldn't stop constructing a ditty based on our mechanic's advice to pinch our tires each day. This we needed to do to determine if they were losing air, as low air pressure requires more pedaling energy. So that morning I had turned to Linda and asked her if she would pinch my tire, to which she replied, with a mischievous twinkle in her eye, "Oh, Sam, I'll pinch your tire any time." I don't think she had my bicycle tire in mind, but I was so tickled by the image that I felt it belonged in a country western song. All along the route, my mind kept turning over possible rhyming possibilities, and, when I hit on one I liked, I kept repeating it over and over and over in hopes I wouldn't forget it. Here's what I came up with:

Y'all started a far (fire)
The day yew (you) first pinched ma (my) tar (tire)
When we biked 'cross country with Bubba
The flame she still burns
My heart she still yearns
For the day when yew first pinched ma tar.

So after dinner I pitched this first stanza to the group to hoots, hollers, laughter, and admonitions not to quit my day job. It was fun.

We bedded down in the Calexico Mission School gym with lights out, and almost every rider out, at nine o'clock.

Sooner or later, something needs to be said about the physical abuse our legs suffer when riding a bicycle. Of course our legs aren't the only part that suffers, and more will be said about the other parts later. There are two huge muscle groups in our legs that do most of the work to make us go forward: the quadriceps and the hamstrings. The quads are on top of the thigh bone and the hamstrings are in back. When we first learned to ride a bike, we had pedals that were flat on top, and the action when pedaling was to push down on the pedal. This we did exclusively with our quads, so they got all the workout. Most recreational bicycles today have flat pedals.

Serious cyclists, however, don't use flat pedals. They have clips on the bottom of their shoes that clip into special pedals, allowing the cyclist to pull up with one leg while pushing down with the other. This pulling up action is done with the hamstrings, resulting in a circular transfer of force as each leg alternatively pulls up and pushes down. There are seven major muscles at work during a cycling outing, and they all work to exhaustion when doing a sixty-mile day in the desert. The result of working muscles hard is their tendency to cramp up.

Cyclists are told to drink a quart of fluids every hour when on the road to keep hydrated, and keeping hydrated is one way, we've been told, to prevent cramping. Fluids containing essential salts, like potassium, are recommended to help in the cramp department as is the ingestion of bananas, another source of potassium. Regardless of how religiously we follow this advice, cramps happen, and when they do the resulting pain is excruciating. When a muscle, and usually it's only one of the seven, tightens from a cramp, the natural reaction is to stretch your leg out straight and turn your toes up. When the muscle relaxes, your tendency is to relax along with it, but as soon as you relax, *zonk!* it tightens up again.

Even though there is a great deal of pain involved, it is quite comical to watch someone experiencing a cramped muscle seizure which we all had the opportunity to do as we slept together in school gymnasia. All will be serene and quiet when suddenly a sleeping bag will erupt and the observant onlooker will hear a muffled, "Oh, no, oh ow, oh God, oh ow, ow, ow" as one corner of the bag shoots out straight. The whispered outburst will be followed by a short period of relaxation when suddenly, "Oh no, not again, oh Jesus, oh yikes, oh ow, ow, ow" as the bag again roils to the agonies experienced therein. Usually cramps don't last but a few minutes, though I've had whole nights with what seemed like each of the tortured seven taking its turn at making me miserable. Even though what we've been told, I don't think anyone knows what causes a cramp. I've asked many physicians and consulted many websites but I have never gotten a definitive answer. It's probably a compendium of low fluids, low electrolytes, extreme stress, and inadequate training. No matter how close attention I paid to my fluid levels nor how much I rode, I was still getting cramps when I tooled into St. Augustine at the end of the journey.

March 10 - Day 4

Calexico CA to Yuma AZ
62 Miles

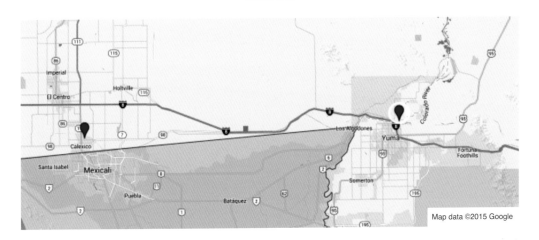

Map data ©2015 Google

I was on the road along with most of the other Coasters by eight after a vegetarian breakfast at seven, again prepared and served by the Calexico Mission School students. Headmistress Smith told us that these students had to get up at three am from their homes in Mexicali to make it to the mission school in time to cook our breakfast. Even though the meals, both dinner and breakfast, were paid for as part of the tour package by Bubba, many of us made a donation to help the school with their finances. As we all left the school compound, we came face to face with our infamous border fence which

Border Fence Right Through the Middle of Calexico

left me feeling somewhat sick to my stomach. I truly believe there can be no peace in the world without justice, and denying people access who truly want to participate in the American dream is unjust. We could work through our differences across the border without the hatred and elitism spawned by this fence.

Once on the road, we faced mile after mile of straight road through the desert. Little by little, the temperature climbed up into the 90s and it seemed an eternity between SAG stops. I pedaled on looking out toward endless vistas of sage brush and sand. The sand belonged to the Imperial Sand Dunes Recreational Area, a favorite site for speeding dune buggies.

Imperial Sand Dunes Recreational Area

When pedaling hour after hour, and without a lot to occupy my mind, it became occupied with complaints from my body which wasn't always feeling all that swift. Today waves of pure agony rose up from my crotch and, even though biking shorts are designed with pads in the crotch to help alleviate this type of pain by spreading out the stresses, they weren't helping me much. It's almost like the pain was caused by a lack of blood in the tissues since once I stood up on my pedals, the blood rushed in and the pain eased. I found I was standing up and pedaling more all the time, an activity our spin instructors insisted we perfect, and it was serving me well by getting me off my bike seat. As soon as I sat down, however, the pain came roaring back. I found too that riding uphill is far easier for me than riding on the flat. Consequently I got to thinking maybe it's because I have more blood rushing into my legs when they're working harder and some gets sidetracked to the aforementioned region.

I found it curious how, as soon as I could find something, anything, to occupy my thoughts, I tended to forget all about my physical complaints. An interesting philosophical question has been posed as to whether pain is "real," the argument being it couldn't be real if one's brain can dismiss it in favor of an interesting preoccupation. I did find my legs were holding up well from the spin classes at the YMCA, but my crotch was becoming more and more distressed as the day wore on. I wasn't having any luck thinking of interesting things to take my mind off it, so, based on this experience, I couldn't avoid the conclusion that pain is, indeed, real.

I did my best to drink enough to keep from getting dehydrated as the sky was cloudless and the sun mercilessly hot. Usually my body doesn't send clear dehydration signals, and I have to force myself to drink, but by the end of the day I was reaching for my water bottle continuously. Speaking of water, every now and again we'd cross a canal weaving it's watery way through the desert. I had seen a few canals the day before, but the closer we got to Yuma and the Arizona border, the more canals we encountered. The landscape too was changing as the sand was giving way to rich farmland, and after about 40 miles along our route, we hit thousands of acres of lettuce, alfalfa, cauliflower and who knows what else growing in perfectly manicured fields. The landscape variety helped to assuage the effects of my physical discomforts, so maybe pain isn't real after all.

We traveled along the shoulder on Interstate 8, having received permission to do so because it was the only road available. Bicycles aren't generally allowed on Interstates, but there was no available access road along the section on which we'd been given permission to ride. Soon we were required to turn off of Interstate 8 because there was an access road into the town of Felicity. This road had to be the worst we Coasters rode on during the whole 2909 miles. The asphalt was torn up with deep ruts between loose chunks of gravel and larger pieces of macadam. It is curious that horribly rough pavement also helps in diverting one's mind from the aches and pains of legs, crotch, and back. Along this access road we jounced and bounced our way for miles until we reached the highlight of the day - a stopover in Felicity to visit the "Center of the World."

Rough Pavement

The story begins with the fellow who invented the para-sail for parachutists, Jacques-Andre Istel. He patented his idea and then made a lot of money selling his products to the military and the world's daredevils. As so often happens with people who make a lot of money, they tend to spend it in interesting, even eccentric, ways. Well, Jacques-Andre decided to build a monument to world history, replete with a pyramid, a chapel, and a history of the world carved in marble prisms covering several acres. The history, chiseled into the triangular prisms in front of the chapel was, as one might suspect, history according to the brains behind the para-sail. Istel's

Oh Really? Who Says?

declared purpose was to leave behind a history of the human race to tell future life forms what was here. I guess we all need something to do after we retire. Even though I was tired from the long, hot, bouncy desert ride, a walk around the prisms to discover which historical events Jacques felt were worth carving into granite was most interesting. It was surprising to me that I'd never heard of the place before Bubba suggested we stop there. I only wish I'd had a day to spend wandering around perusing Jacques' take on history. I'll leave it up to the reader to "Google" why the place is called the Center of the World instead of the Middle of Nowhere.

Chapel with History Prisms in Foreground

From the Center of the World, we crossed the Arizona border, the second state on our tour. Below are Jeff and Lisa Arndt standing under a

Jeff & Lisa Entering Arizona

welcome sign from a state that is known for being perhaps the least welcoming in the country if you happen to be Latino. Note that Jeff is wearing white pullovers covering his arms and legs, which might seem odd with the temperatures in the 90s. Jeff was probably the strongest and possibly the most experienced rider in the group, and he said the thin white cloth actually helped him stay cool as it kept the hot sun off his skin.

Anyway, on to Yuma. Yuma is a lovely town on the Colorado River with three claims to fame: military history, agriculture, and tourism. There was a large military base in Yuma during WWII that was scheduled to close after the war. However, Yumans (Yumaonians?), with the Army's assistance, staged the longest continuous airplane flight ever made from the Yuma Army base. The plane flew with two pilots for fifty-five days, skimming low over the airbase runway to pick up groceries and gasoline from a speeding convertible. This evidently impressed somebody in a position of authority, as the airbase was left open providing a large measure of revenue to the local economy. As one might imagine, with the desert so close at hand, a great deal of troop training for the Iraq war was done in Yuma. So important is the military presence in Yuma that the Arizona National Guard built a beautiful new gymnasium overlooking the city where we Coasters spent the night.

In addition to the military presence, agriculture and tourism are both essential to the economy of the city. Ninety-five percent of all winter vegetables in grocery stores across the country come from Yuma. The growing season is continuous, and the Colorado River supplies all the necessary water. To support tourism, the Yuma City Council restored the Colorado river banks and converted the old prison into a museum. At one time the high school burned down, so the prison, abandoned at the time, was used as the high school until a new one could be built. As a result, the moniker for the home team is the Criminals, and the football team is now escorted out to the playing field behind police squad cars. It's a nice historical touch.

I was exhausted from the heat and the ten miles of rough road leading to the Center of the World ,so as soon as I got to the gym, I flopped on my mattress and slept for an hour before dinner. Naps after a long ride had become an essential interlude in my routine during this trip.

March 11 - Day 5

Yuma to Dateland
70 Miles

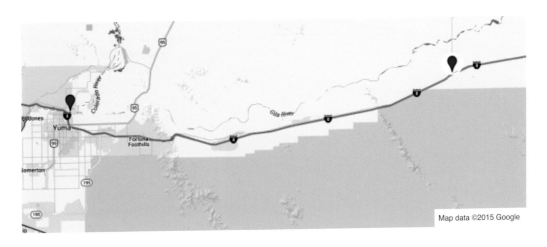

Map data ©2015 Google

We awoke to a resplendent rose-colored sunrise with the sailor's adage, "Red sun in the morning, sailors take warning," raising concerns for the day's prospects of rain. Nevertheless, Coasters scrambled for their cameras to get the shot of the crimson horizon before it vanished with the dawn. While cameras clicked away, a voice in the throng said, "Just Google, 'sunrise photos.' You'll probably find it there." This brought a chuckle from those scrambling, but it didn't slow them down. The day began cool, though, very cool for Yuma, and the sun didn't ever break through the clouds until well after noon. Fortunately the adage hadn't been proven scientifically as it never did rain.

The first leg of our daily jaunt took us through some of the most amazing agricultural fields imaginable. Try to picture 640 acres of iceberg lettuce, lying next to 640 acres of cauliflower, which adjoined 640 acres of romaine. Six hundred forty acres is a Section according to the Public Land Survey System and represents one square mile. Each field was perfectly flat and perfectly manicured without a weed in sight. The product in several of the fields was being harvested, and it appeared that all the workers in the fields were Latinos. America has had a long history of importing

Caesar Salad, Anyone?

bracero workers from Mexico, and why we ever discontinued our migrant worker program is a mystery to me. Clearly the fact that there is no longer a bracero program doesn't discourage the farm owners or the Latinos from finding a way to continue this long history.

The harvesting we saw along our bike route was done by hand. Some of the product was put immediately into boxes for shipment, and some was put on specially designed trailers pulled slowly along by tractors. These trailers covered several rows with the workers following along behind. The laborers were all very friendly, standing up and

smiling and waving when we stopped to take their pictures. The work was back-breaking as it required constant bending at the waist, so it wasn't surprising they took any opportunity to stand up and stretch their muscles. At one field a supervisor waved us off and didn't allow any pictures to be taken. I can only assume some (most?) of his field hands were undocumented. We took the pictures anyway, knowing there was no way they would fall into the wrong hands.

Harvesting by Hand

Canals filled to the brim with water criss-crossed the terrain, and I was told the fields were all laid out at gentle angles (whoops, guess they weren't perfectly flat, but they looked flat!) so that they could be flooded and excess water could run off. I did see pumps and some sprinklers, but they were few and far between. As I rode along, trucks passed by continuously, leaving the fields loaded with produce. Seeing all this productive agricultural land made me wonder what the land looked like before it was planted with cabbages. I soon found out as little by little the landscape turned from agriculture to desert. This left me with the impression fertile soil lay just below the sand surface and all one had to do was plow up the desert to create another 640 acre breadbasket.

Land Before the Plow

Once out of the agricultural district, we hit desert and more desert with the road disappearing in a straight line to the all-too-familiar distant vanishing point. We passed several wide spots in the road sporting nothing more than a single market or gas station. We stopped for lunch in Welton, one of the widest spots in the road we encountered all day. Jac's Whistle Stop Cafe was usually closed on Wednesday but stayed open just for us cyclists who probably gave Jac more business in one day than he usually got in a week. I remember sitting outside with others and eating my neighbor's fries.

From lunch, as we biked east. Our road paralleled the railroad where trains came down the tracks in both directions at frequent intervals. Linda and I had fun waving madly at the lead engines hoping to garner the attention of the engineer so that he'd blow his whistle for us. Some did blow their whistles and we usually scored about a fifty percent success rate. The trains were all carrying either ocean shipping containers or automobiles, though

Jac's Whistle Stop Cafe

occasionally we would see a tank car or empty flatbed. Knowing that every container kept an eighteen-wheeler off the interstate was comforting for those of us who were conscious of our carbon footprint.

Dateland Truck Stop and RV Camp

One last insult to the quiet prairie was a beef feed lot that I saw which seemed to go on for miles. In the distance behind the lot were three grain silos, next to which was what appeared to be a mountain of corn. In the foreground, penned up with little room to move, were thousands of mooing critters, all destined for a MacDonald's or Carl's Jr. Surrounding the feed lot were neatly coiffed rows of cow manure drying in the hot desert sun. I'll probably be buying bags of this at Agway come spring.

Late in the afternoon Linda and I arrived in Dateland which seemed to be little more than a Texaco station, fast food restaurant, curio shop, and RV camp. I expected vast orchards of date palms, and I'm sure they existed somewhere, as I'm sure the center of town existed somewhere, but the RV park where we stopped certainly wasn't in the middle of a forest of palms nor was it close to any signs of a grander civilization. Our campsite just happened to be right next to the train tracks, so it was a night punctuated by the sounds of a country on the move. There is something eerily romantic about a train whistle in the middle of the night, and somehow this romanticism takes the edge off the aggravation of being awakened. It cooled off a lot that night, and by morning the temperature was in the low fifties. The temperature would be climbing as the day progressed, and the cool temperatures helped our bodies cope with the exertions that lay ahead.

Bubba Dome Tent City in Dateland

March 12 - Day 6

Dateland to Gila Bend
53 Miles

Map data ©2015 Google

Linda and I started at dawn on one of the roughest frontage roads we'd bounced down since heading for the Center of the World. Frontage roads, especially if rarely used thanks to the interstate, get pretty low priority for routine maintenance. For twelve miles we banged, and chattered down loose gravel between chunks of asphalt. The road ran right along the tracks, and as each loaded train roared by, we did our thing and waived frantically at the engineer. Once our required twelve-mile penance was traversed, the frontage road came to an end, and we were able to return to the shoulder of the Interstate.

However safe interstates may seem, one problem when riding along the shoulder is the accumulation of semi-trailer retread refuse. These are the large bands of rubber that tear off a semi tire at high speed and wind up alongside the road. These retreads are laced with very small steel wires that can, (and do at alarming regularity,) lodge themselves in a bicycle tire. They then work their way through the tire and into the inner tube and *Bingo!* you have a flat. Changing a flat along a busy interstate where traffic, especially in Arizona, is traveling at speeds well in excess of the seventy mph speed limit is certainly dangerous. Nevertheless, I would rather ride down a wide interstate shoulder than a narrow rural road with heavy logging truck traffic and no shoulder. We had some of these and they could be heart stopping at times.

The first SAG stop set up this day was an official interstate rest area, but there were a number of red and yellow plastic cans in front of the off ramp, indicating it was closed. Bubba instructed us all to pull into the stop anyway, since he had gained permission from the appropriate authorities for us to SAG there. It was a lovely rest area with toilets and picnic tables neatly laid out in a southwestern style worthy of Arizona. I couldn't fathom why the rest area was closed as it seemed to be in good shape and had clean, functioning restrooms. Unfortunately the authority from whom Bubba received approval for us to ignore the cans hadn't made the effort to communicate his decision to others who might be

involved, and a state park officer stopped by to make a few inquiries. He was not a happy camper, but his mood was mollified somewhat with the knowledge that Bubba was a retired law officer himself and had received permission from higher authorities to use the site. All's well that ends well.

Murph Making Sure We All Used Hand Sanitizer

After the twelve miles of disastrous road we were required to ride prior to getting to this stop, our bike mechanic, Chandler, spun everyone's wheels to see if they still ran true. Some of us had had problems with broken spokes, and these were replaced by Chandler who had to take the wheel off the bike and the tire and tube off the wheel to perform the operation. Fortunately most of us had taken Chandler's advice and brought extra spokes with us for use in just such emergencies.

The desert went on and on and on; ten, twenty, and thirty miles unfolded with absolutely nothing but sagebrush, bushes with yellow flowers nobody (me?) knew the name of, and Saguaro cactus. Saguaro is tall, multi-armed cactus notable for depictions of tired Mexicans snoozing at their bases with sombreros pulled over their eyes and serapes draped over their shoulders. It's a rather sad depiction as I never saw anyone work harder than the Mexicans we saw harvesting salad greens in the Imperial Valley. Note the big silver train cars in the background. These cars carry automobiles, and I was surprised how much of the train traffic in the south is devoted to moving automobiles around.

Saguaro, Me and the Train

This part of America is known as the Sonoran Desert, a land area that covers 100,000 square miles. It challenges the Mojave Desert's Death Valley as the hottest place in America and is the only place where the aforementioned Saguaro cactus grows. It is home to mountain lions, and it is the ancestral home of seventeen Native American tribes. From the hot seat of a twenty-four speed bicycle, it is hard to appreciate all the history and lore of the desert, but there is no question the casual observer has to be moved to awe by the serene beauty of its immense majesty. I loved the desert, though I was happy to be passing through it to get to the lush green tropics on the other side.

One of the interesting sights I saw as I pedaled along were fields of black, porous boulders. These boulders all looked like they had just blown out of a volcano. And, sure enough, though there wasn't volcano in sight, geologists have found significant evidence of volcanic activity in the past. Presumably these boulders were eventually covered up by a vast inland sea whose sand sediments buried them until the present day. As the sand erodes away driven by the dual forces of wind and rain, the boulders make their appearance on the surface.

Forty miles from Dateline the landscape turned suddenly green, hundreds and thousands of acres of green. It could easily have been silage for use in the cattle feed lots. Our route again took us across canals filled with water presumably syphoned off the Gila River to slake the thirst of whatever was growing in the fields. Next to the canals and spread out across the landscape loomed a huge solar farm, built by a Spanish company, to heat oil pumped through parabolic arrays aimed at the sun. The oil then transferred its heat to a steam turbine-powered electric generator, which sent its output to southern California. We learned at a presentation made to the group at Gila Bend that the plant was an economic success, belying the claim that solar power will never be competitive. Eventually I am certain we will produce vast quantities of electric power economically, and certainly there will be no better place to generate it than the Sonoran Desert where the, "skies are not cloudy all day."

Friendly Gila Bend

It wasn't a long day, so most of us were in Gila Bend by noon, stopping at Sophia's Mexican Restaurant for lunch before entering the city. Judging from the sign, it's not much of a city, but at least they think of themselves as friendly and have their crabs identified. It made me wonder if the crabs used to be friendly, but years of living in Gila Bend made them crabs. Maybe in a few years there will be five friendly people and seventeen hundred crabs.

Mobile America

Once entering the "city" we headed right to Augie's Quail Trail RV Park where the temperature was nudging one hundred degrees. Augie's was a huge park laid out mostly for the benefit of recreational vehicles. There were one hundred thirty two spaces for those who wish to turtle their homes around behind them, and while the park wasn't full, there sure were a lot of RVs there. Space can be rented for $280 a month, which must make it an attractive alternative to real estate taxes on a house. Many of the RVs were towing cars so one can come, park their mobile house in a space, and then tour the surrounding countryside in their cars. Some of the cars were almost as big as the RVs. This type of life is one that holds absolutely no appeal for me, but we saw so many RV parks during our trek, that the appeal certainly is widespread.

There was a very nice communal center at Augie's with sufficient air conditioning to make it an attractive gathering place for us weary cyclists. It is amazing that no matter how much we enjoyed being removed from the crush of everyday events while cycling, as soon as the cycling day came to a close many rushed to their iPhones, iPads and Laptops to get back in touch. To do this at Augie's, we assembled in the communal center close to wall outlets, plugged in our devices and proceeded to log onto the park's "high speed" internet connection. The "high" in high speed, it turned out, was dependent on the amount of traffic on the system, the more people who logged on, the slower it became. There were enough of us logged on at one point to reduce "high" to practically non-existent. The frustration level in the communal center was palpable as we waited for screens to refresh, tapped our fingers, and rolled our eyes at our comrades. I became sufficiently frustrated to walk the several hundred yards to Augie's office to complain, but, when I arrived, I met a perfectly delightful lady who gave me the password to the office internet server - a server that worked great as I was the only one using it.

There isn't much grass in Gila Bend, so the area set aside for tents was located on crushed rock. Crushed rock is supposed to deter the movement of rattle snakes, but it plays havoc with the bottoms of one's feet as pieces of stone lodge in one's flip-

Augie's Office

flops. The ground is hard as well, so the crew setting up the tents was having a devil of a time pounding the tent stakes, huge nails actually, into the ground. To make matters more interesting an evening breeze had picked up, and the wind was whipping the tent flaps around. The whipping flaps dislodged the tent nails not hammered sufficiently deep into the hardpan. This kept the support crew busy finding new spots to hammer in the nails while holding flapping flaps to keep them from flapping while they hammered.

After dinner, Bubba had arranged a presentation about the history of Arizona. Do you remember (I know we were all supposed to learn it in seventh grade) that the Gadsden Purchase was bought for the benefit of the Southern Pacific Railroad so that the trains wouldn't have to traverse any mountains? As a cyclist, this was a rationale with which I could easily identify. It was interesting to learn, also, that from the time the land in the Imperial Valley was first farmed, the farmers in California, Arizona, and Mexico argued over water rights. To ease tensions, the states made an agreement to parcel out the available water to impacted parties by acre-feet. However, something got lost in translation, and there never has been enough water in the Colorado or the Gila for anyone to get their allotted share. Though nobody has ever gotten their agreed upon share, everyone believes that everyone else is getting theirs so tensions remain. The real loser has been Mexico, since most of the water in both rivers is siphoned off to American agribusiness long before it makes its way to Mexico.

March 13 - Day 7

Gila Bend to Casa Grande
79 Miles

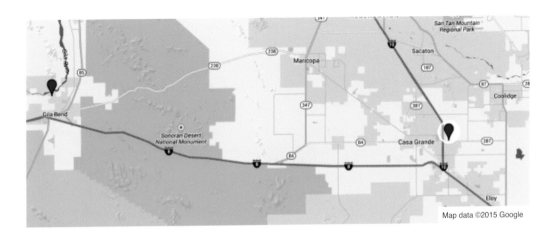

Map data ©2015 Google

Another day dawned in the Sonoran Desert with temperatures in the high fifties. I headed east out of Augie's immediately after breakfast to get a jump on the seventy-nine miles we had to ride that day. The desert seemed endless as I pedaled and pedaled and pedaled alongside sand, sagebrush and Saguaro cactus. I stopped to check out a description of the desert just as John pulled in and we took each other's pictures in front of the sign. There wasn't much else of which to take pictures. The morning ride was lovely with good roads, little traffic, and calm winds. I stopped for refreshments after 25 miles at the first SAG stop, and then took off again. The wind started to pick up and, *rats,* it was right in my face. There was also a rather long climb to begin the day, so between the headwind and the climb, I was sure to be tired when I hit Casa Grande. My fatigue was accelerated by the hot sun as I lost body fluids during my pedaling exertions. They say a cyclist is supposed to drink a quart an hour, but I didn't and didn't know anyone else who did. I found it fascinating that my body was losing fluids but it was not sending any signals to my brain to drink more. Those signals all came flooding in after I was

Author in the Sonoran Desert

through for the day, and then I could drink three diet cokes and a quart of chocolate milk without stopping to breathe. Chocolate milk, by the way, is a wonderful thirst quencher and protein replacement mechanism.

One of the problems we encountered was cracking skin, especially lips, so Linda decided to wear a Mexican bandana across her nose and mouth to protect her lips from direct sunlight and from blowing sand. I enjoyed calling her Señora Bandita, but I couldn't get the namesake to stick among the other riders.

Linda is a resident of Oaxaca, Mexico where she owns a bed and breakfast, Casa Linda, in the foothills overlooking the city. Every year on December 12th Linda holds a special gathering of ladies to celebrate the appearance of the Virgin of Guadalupe, A.K.A Virgin Mary, to the

Señora Bandita

peasant Juan Diego. The Virgin came to Juan in a vision at the Hill of Tepeyac on

Virgin of Guadalupe

December 12th, 1531 and asked that a cathedral be built on the hill. Señor Diego, being a good servant of the Lord, went immediately to Archbishop Fray Juan de Zumárraga in Mexico City and relayed the message. The tolerant and understanding archbishop wanted some additional signal from the Virgin, so he sent Juan back to reconnect with the Virgin, and, more than likely, forgot all about him. Juan returned to the spot where the Virgin told him to build the cathedral, and there she waited, no doubt somewhat ticked off at the archbishop for his lack of faith. She advised Juan to climb the hill and fill his apron with roses, roses that had never grown there prior to, and go back to the archbishop and show him what he had found. When Juan opened his apron in front of Archbishop Fray Juan de Zamáragga, not only was it full of gorgeous red roses, but the cloak itself carried the image at the left. The archbishop was convinced, and The Basilica of Our Lady of Guadalupe now stands on the site.

To commemorate this miraculous vision, Linda gathers her Oaxacan lady friends together to construct facsimiles on wooded forms out of whatever material they happen to bring with them or whatever Linda happens to provide. Individual creativity is encouraged with few guidelines, other than that the figure must be female and must radiate rays of light signifying the Virgin's pure inner core. The results are whimsical, colorful, and wonderfully imaginative. Some of their creations are shown in the picture on the following page.

You're of course wondering where I'm going with this. Well, at our first SAG stop this day, Linda and I got to talking about all the really neat stuff that was discharged along

Virgins of Guadalupe from Linda's Lady's Day

the side of the road, and she came up with the suggestion that we begin collecting it to use to make a Roadside Virgin of Guadalupe we could to present to Bubba at the end of the tour. It would serve as Bubba's Road Bike Patron Saint ostensibly with the power to protect the riders under his care and supervision. As we relayed this idea to other riders, we stirred their interest, and many started to look for roadside treasures. Once we started looking, it was absolutely amazing what turned up. By the end of the tour we had collected forty-eight different items that Linda and friends made into Bubba's virgin, presenting it to him on our last rest day at the O'Leno State Park in Florida.

Toward noon, the wind blew in our faces, the road got narrower, and the truck traffic picked up, making me well aware of staying as far to the side of the road as possible. The posted limit was seventy-five, which seemed to be interpreted by most drivers to go as fast as their vehicles would allow. Some cars passed me at what seemed to be speeds approaching a hundred. There wasn't much to see, but I did witness what could be the world's largest landfill in the middle of the desert. I imagine trash from both Phoenix and Tucson came to this site, which looked like a flat topped mountain towering over the desert landscape. Landfills just have a "look" that is easily identifiable.

Once through Maricopa, I passed a facility full of beef critters with a sign indicating the facility was a dairy. Next to it was the biggest feed lot I'd ever seen (and I'd just seen a huge one a few days ago) with steers penned up waiting for their turn at McDonald's. I suppose it makes sense to put a facility full of cows capable of producing steers next to a facility for fattening them up for slaughter, but the sight of these poor animals penned up day and night was indeed disquieting. These dairy and

Really Big Feed Lot

feed lot operations loomed like an oasis out of the Sahara for as soon as they appeared, they were gone and the desert returned.

Our destination for the day was Casa Grande, an agricultural center with a present day population of 50,000 established as a terminus for the Southern Pacific Railroad in 1880 with five citizens and two buildings. In fact it was originally called Terminus, but its name was later changed to Casa Grande after the Hohokam Native American ruins nearby. Casa Grande means Big House in Spanish, and one of the Hohokam ruins was indeed a big house. We didn't have the time to visit these ruins, but they would have been an interesting side trip. The Hohokam resided in the Sonoran Desert in the 13th century, building irrigation canals and farming the rich soils just as is done today. I found all the Spanish names we kept encountering in this part of America a telling example of how integrated our two cultures were in the not too distant past.

This night Bubba arranged for us to stay in the gymnasium of the Casa Grande Vista Grande High School, where the State Champion Indoor Percussion Ensemble was practicing when most of us arrived. We were therefore denied access to the gymnasium upon arrival and, as a consequence, denied access to our blown up air mattresses, a luxury I, in particular, relished as I couldn't wait to lie down and take my requisite nap before dinner. However, it was a hoot to see fellow cyclists sacked out on benches, snoozing in plastic chairs, and curled up on the concrete waiting for the ensemble to wind up their drumming so we could move in.

Dinner was cooked and served by students studying in the school's culinary arts program and consisted of lasagna, tossed salad, and trifle for dessert. They were a lovely group of kids; poised, polite, and ambitious to make something of their lives.

This day had been the longest day yet, and I was feeling it in my legs and groin. We'll have another seventy-miler on the day following, and I was oh-so-ready to turn in as soon as dinner was over. About half us cyclists spent the night in the gym, while the other half took their air mattresses outside where it was cooler, cooler to start anyway. I stayed in the gym and was glad I did since cool turned to cold by morning and I wouldn't have had enough covers to keep warm. Being used to New England summers teeming with blood sucking bugs, it's hard for me to forget my childhood at camp sleeping outside and being swarmed by insects. There is absolutely nothing that interrupts my sleep more than a mosquito buzzing around my ear in the middle of the night. I wouldn't mind if they just dropped in, extracted their drop of blood, and then flew off without that infernal *zzzzzz*. But, as I said, the night cooled off and mosquitoes might not have survived the morning cold. Still and all it was the fear of bugs, not the fear of being cold, that kept me inside.

Roadside pickup today was a **Stuffed Toy Rabbit**

March 14 - Day 8
Casa Grande to Santa Catalina State Park
72 Miles

Map data ©2015 Google

The culinary crew at the Vista Grande High School fixed a wonderful breakfast: piles of scrambled eggs, mountains of English muffins, and platters of heaped bacon. I attacked the eggs and bacon because the body burns protein before it burns fat to satisfy its energy requirements, and, remembering Sophia Loren, I stayed away from the English muffins. Of course, the body's metabolism isn't so simple, as I was to find out as our journey progressed. When I started out, I expected to lose all my belly fat, and I expected it to melt off rather quickly. As a rough guide we read that the body needs 1,500 calories a day to run itself whether we exercise or not, and that we'll lose weight if we just feed it less than 1,500 a day. As mentioned previously, when on a bike our bodies burn through about fifty to sixty calories a mile. At fifty miles a day our body will require

Sam

2,500 additional calories. Wow, I thought, if I just eat less than 4,000 calories a day, goodbye belly fat. Well, that didn't happen. I did lose weight, but the dreaded "love handles" remained probably because Anne's cooking was so good that I downed more than 4,000 calories at each sitting. It's great to be a cycling foodie because it's almost impossible to eat too much. You might not lose any fat, but you'll have plenty of energy to pedal up that next rise.

Mornings in the desert were glorious and I headed east on smooth roads, cool temperatures, clear skies, and calm winds. The restorative powers of a good night's sleep overwhelmed me and I sang "Home on the Range" at the top of my lungs as I rode along. After about twenty-five miles an east wind began and, contrary to what I was led to believe about prevailing winds blowing west to east, this wind hit me head-on. Soon I had lost all interest in making the range my home as I bent forward on my handlebars trying to minimize my body resistance; blinked my eyes to relieve them of the grit sneaking in under my glasses; and steeled my body against sideways gusts blowing me off balance. Cycling has many aggravations based on weather, terrain, equipment, and physical conditioning, but from my perspective wind is absolutely the worst, and it's worst by a large margin. First it slows me down, so I get frustrated by working hard and not going anywhere. At least if I'm biking uphill, I can anticipate an exhilarating downhill sometime in my future, but I'd been cycling in Mexico in a headwind and had to pedal in low gear to go downhill. It's no fun. And, of course, the direction of the wind isn't constant. It's always shifting from side to side, slow to fast, so the cyclist must be continually alert to being blown off balance. Finally, when in the desert, there is the blowing dust and sand which coated my face, arms, and legs such that when I stopped I felt like I'd been rolling in a mud pit. This is what we faced heading for Santa Catalina State Park, and we faced it hour after hour, agonizing mile after agonizing mile.

Picacho Peak in the Distance

And Awesome They Were

I'd seen Picacho Peak as a speck in the distance when I started out, and I'd been straining toward it, head bowed into the wind, for hours and hours through a Saguaro Cacti-littered landscape. It was a relief to finally get to Picacho Peak and realize I could stock up on "Awesome" souvenirs. Well, there wasn't room on the bikes to carry much, but the sign lived up to it's reputation. It was the most well-stocked store of curios and mementos I'd ever seen. It was stocked with the largest aviary of carved Bald Eagles you could imagine, all with fierce, penetrating eyes. These were displayed together with Native American ornamentation of every description: knives, bows, arrows, headdresses and jewelry. A machismo rig driver could drive away with a stuffed buffalo head strapped to the grille of his Peterbilt eighteen-wheeler, and, along with this wild west statement, he could proudly wear a t-shirt radiating his fealty to the Second Amendment by stating the twelve reasons why hand guns are better than women.

And here they are, some are actually quite funny:

1. You can buy a silencer for a hand gun
2. You can trade your .44 in for two .22's.
3. You can have one hand gun at home and another for the road.
4. If you admire a friend's hand gun, and tell him so, he will be impressed and let you try it out.
5. Your handgun will stay with you even if you're out of ammo.
6. Your primary handgun doesn't mind if you have a backup.
7. Handguns don't take up a lot of closet space.
8. Handguns function normally every day of the month.
9. A handgun won't ask, "Do these grips make me look fat?"
10. A handgun doesn't mind if you go to sleep right after you're done using it.
11. A handgun doesn't care how big your trigger finger is.
12. A handgun doesn't complain if you are a little fast on the trigger.

Fortunately, Picacho Peak Plaza was home to a Dairy Queen where I slaked my thirst with a root beer float and a giant soft ice-cream. These I slurped and licked very slowly as the thought of re-entering the wind and the dust wasn't exactly my idea of a good time. Eventually my treats were gone, and I went headlong into the wind for another thirty miles.

Santa Catalina State Park, located ten miles north of Tucson, contained vast array of desert plants, wildlife and archeological sites in a 5,500-acre, high-desert park. There were more than 150 species of birds who call the park home, and I saw many hikers with ponderous binoculars, floppy hats, walking sticks, and backpacks ambling along the trails. Obviously they were birders. Birders just have this "look" about them, a different "look" than landfills, fortunately, but still a "look." There was also an equestrian center and miles of riding trails through the adjoining Coronado National Forest. The facilities at the park were exemplary and the setting simply spectacular. This was surely the toughest day so far, and looking back, I think it was the toughest day of the entire C2C. It was the combination of miles of climbing into the wind and fighting off dust devils that made it so. My legs were absolutely dead.

See the Anthill in Front of My Tent?

As I prepared to crash for my nap, I discovered a mound of fire ants right at the entrance. These are nasty critters and their bites sting horribly, so the last thing I wanted was to wake up in the middle of the night covered in fire ants. Actually, I understand the Native Americans used to bury their victims up to the neck next to a fire ant mound. This would surely be a tough way to go and might have given pause to the way we assimilated with the indigenous peoples if the Commissioners of Indian Affairs faced such treatments for their relocation decisions. Not wanting to suffer in the middle of the night, I notified our support staff about the ants in front of my tent, and it was from them I learned that Clorox is an effective agent for dispersing fire ants. I don't know if they ran off to live somewhere else or all curled into a ball and turned white, but it didn't matter to me. They were gone after an appropriate application. I couldn't believe I'd been alive for seventy-two years and never heard of this anti-ant remedy.

The evening turned out to be one of the most spectacular of the entire trip. First there was no moonlight to interfere with light from the distant heavens as the moon was a waning crescent moon, which wouldn't be visible until morning. Then the temperature had dropped and the wind had died leaving the air clear enough for the Milky Way to be easily discernible as a swath of heavenly sparklers showering their crystals on the serene desert.

As I gazed up at the stars this night of March 14, I felt extremely lucky to be alive.

Roadside pickup today was a **Man's Nike Hightop Tennis Shoe**

March 15 - Day 9

Santa Catalina State Park
Rest Day

Glorious Crescent Moon Early in the Morning

I awoke early the next morning and witnessed the crescent moon as it rose over the mountains. It was another awesome sight. I needed a good day of rest and this state park was a beautiful place to do just that. Since this was a rest day, breakfast was served late so those who wanted to sleep in could do so. It was around ten am before our group got into their day's activities. A few of us were up for a hike around the hills, but others

chose to go to the modern shopping center a couple of miles away. We were advised to keep our eyes peeled for rattlesnakes, and this deterred some of us from venturing too far away from camp. The advice was well placed as, sure enough, a rattler was seen right next to the rest rooms where we all walked in flip-flops to take our showers. One of our group snapped a photo before calling a park ranger who ushered it back to the wilds. I just really, really don't like rattlesnakes. Actually, all snakes give me the willies,

Oh Dear Me!

and I'm partial to the sentiments expressed by the fat lady in the comic strip BC who throttles any snake she sees. I know, I know, it's not very understanding of the important place snakes play in the grand scheme of things orchestrated by Mother Nature, but hey, I'm not about to challenge my dislike of snakes by trying to befriend them. The demonstrated presence of rattlers in our camp surroundings lent slipping out to the rest room in the middle of the night an extra measure of heart-thumping excitement to our cycling adventure, especially for the women. Most of us senior men had a quart G2 bottle in our tents we used when the urge struck at night ,which it did to me quite frequently. The very thought of stepping on a rattler in the dark, feeling it wiggle under my foot, hearing its telltale buzz, and then getting injected with a dose of venom in the calf makes me shiver all over even as I write this.

If you want to dazzle friends with your knowledge of nature, you can ask them if they knew there were no poisonous snakes in Arizona. If they are especially sure of themselves and express strong disbelief, citing rattlesnakes and copperheads and maybe even gila monsters, make them a bet; the bigger the better. Then go to Google and learn that, in fact, snakes and gila monsters are not poisonous, they're venomous. Poison works through the digestive system whereas venom works through the circulatory system, primarily the lymph nodes. Maybe you'll make enough to pay for this book. By the way, thank you for buying it. Lisa and Jeff thank you as well.

Since there weren't any bicycling adventures to write about on this rest day, this is a good place introduce the types of bikes we Coasters were riding from coast to coast.

Standard 24 Speed Road Bike

As this was a trip to be taken along paved roads, the most common bike was the multi-speed, upright "road bike." These bikes are characterized by narrow tires containing rubber inner tubes pumped up to over one hundred psi pressure. The high pressure makes them fast on good roads, which is nice, but the high pressure also transmits every variation in road surface to your molars so they aren't very rider friendly on rough roads. There are from twenty to twenty-seven gear changes available on these road bikes, depending on how many chain rings there are. All shifting is conveniently done from levers on the handle bars.

Frames are made from steel, titanium, aluminum, carbon fiber, and even wood if you can believe it. Steel is heavy but stiff and some people prefer a stiff frame. Titanium is light and stiff, whereas aluminum is light and flexible, as is carbon fiber. And wood, well, I saw a wooden frame in a bike shop in California that was a thing of rare beauty, but nobody had one on this C2C. I imagine it would be light and flexible, but I might be a bit nervous about wear and tear over time.

I've already mentioned clip-in pedals. There are several different types of clip-in pedals and they all take some getting used to. The first mistake made by all cyclists is forgetting to unclip their shoe at a stop. The result is they fall over on their knee, break the skin, and feel really, really stupid, especially if others are watching... and laughing. The new rider will fall three times and then never forget to unclip again as long as he shall live.

One personal variable is the seat, from which there are a myriad of types and styles to choose. My own experience is they are all comfy at the start of a ride but become less and less comfy as the ride progresses. The solution is to do so much riding that all the nerve endings in your crotch die off and your skin down there turns to alligator hide. By the time we reached St. Augustine I no longer suffered any discomfort, but at the start of the ride, yikes, I was in torment most of the time.

Most of us carried our water in water bottles in brackets on the frame, but some had Camel-Backs", a water bladder worn on one's back with a tube positioned close to one's mouth from which to draw water. We all ported differing styles of bike packs to carry spare parts, rain jackets, snacks, and anything else felt to be worth the extra weight.

John's BIG BLUE Recumbent

Sitting upright for hours at a time on a seat too small for comfort isn't everyone's cup of tea, so enter the two wheel recumbent bike. These bikes are designed for those with back problems aggravated by hours sitting bent forward on an upright bike. John was an experienced cyclist, and when his back and shoulders began to bother him from too many hours on an upright bicycle, he tried a recumbent cycle and it suited him perfectly. Recumbents have the same gearing as upright bikes, but they are heavier and require a different pedaling action. Note the front wheel is smaller than the rear wheel, making it necessary to carry two different sizes of spare inner tubes. John had a faring put on the front of his bike to streamline it, and the faring did its job, as John was a very fast rider. We had two recumbents on the trip.

We then had three tricycles with two wheels in front and one in the rear. These are recumbent vehicles that offer the rider an added measure of stability. The pedals are in front but the drive chain runs down the spine of the bike and is connected to the rear wheel. They are reputed to be very comfortable, but they sit low to the ground and are so hard to see that all riders have a flag pole attached to the back to make them more visible. Ken had a trike equipped with an electric motor and lithium battery so he could choose a bit of a boost at any time. He took great delight in peeling out from SAG stops,

Ken's Battery Powered Tricycle

leaving everyone in his dust and then, when his battery ran out of juice on the next long hill, everyone took great delight in leaving him in their dust. He had two batteries that he charged at night, putting one in his trike in the morning and leaving the second with the SAG team for changing out later in the day. The biggest problem with trikes is their width. On a two lane road without a shoulder there wasn't enough room for two cars and a trike in the lanes provided, and Coach had some awfully close calls with logging trucks as they tried to pass his trike in the presence of oncoming traffic and chose to run the road on several occasions realizing a collision was imminent from an overtaking truck. Bubba decided at the end of the tour it was the last year he was going to allow tricycles. They just weren't safe enough.

Coach's Standard Tricycle

Randy and Colleen's Tandem

Finally, Randy and Colleen chose to make the ride across the country on a tandem bike. They were a unique couple since Randy was almost blind, and needed Colleen to ride in front to pick out the route. Colleen radiated charm coupled with a quiet competence, and it was easy to understand Randy's devotion. What confidence they had in each other's abilities to even undertake this great American traverse, yet they did it pumping out the miles every day just like the rest of us.

I took a nap when I returned from my rest day spent at Best Buy where I worked on my blog. I then took a shower before the evening meal. As dark descended, Bubba fashioned a campfire and a number of us sat around telling bicycling stories. It was extremely pleasant, and I stayed a while after the group had headed for bed, again dazzled by the heavenly light show overhead pondering the miracle and mystery of life on earth. Buddhists believe all life in the universe is connected and, as we learn the lessons we need to learn about compassion, loving kindness, and understanding on Earth as humans, we will be reincarnated on other planets where there will more lessons to learn. Looking up at the billions of twinkling overhead lights, it was easy to imagine many planets capable of supporting life in fulfillment of the Buddha's vision.

March 16 - Day 10
Santa Catalina State Park to Tucson
43 Miles

We Coasters arose at dawn to anther glorious clear sky with the same (well not quite) crescent moon hanging over the mountains. It was cold and everyone was bundled up at breakfast. We had oatmeal and real maple syrup. Few seemed to have grown up with a palate sensitized to the delights of real maple syrup, as I seemed to be the only one who used any. I used a lot on my oatmeal, cream too.

Bike Path in Tucson

One by one, we then headed south to the Tucson city limits and then through the city itself. The first part of the ride was wonderful as Tucson and its northern environs are extremely bicycle-friendly. We pedaled down lovely bike trails, through quiet neighborhoods, and along sandy arroyos on newly asphalted surfaces. The wind was calm, the temperatures cool, and the morning sun reflected brilliantly off red tile, subdivision rooftops. I didn't sing "Home on the Range," but my soul soared enough to do so. What a beautiful start to a magnificent day.

We had one interesting situation where Ken's electric trike was too wide for one of the bike trail gates. As cyclists backed up behind him, he soon had enough willing hands to lift the machine, turn it sideways and usher it through the bottleneck.

To the south of Tucson resides the largest airplane graveyard in the world. There are thousands of aircraft in mothballs just sitting in the desert. Whether they are ready to fly or not is anybody's guess, but engines, doors, windows, and all apertures are covered in shrink wrap to protect moving parts from the fine dust that permeates everything. It wouldn't surprise me if the shrink wrapping didn't keep all the dust out of sensitive places, and I'd hate to be the pilot of a plane just taken out of mothballs.

Ken Through the Gate

Shrink Wrapped C-130 Cargo Planes

Once past the graveyard, I turned off to visit the Pima Air and Space Museum. It was quite a site with old airplanes of every size and shape. The coolest exhibit was a real live SR-71 Blackbird, a plane that used to fly out of the airbase in California close to my home. The pilots would have a quiet breakfast with their wives and children, spend the day at mach-3 over the Soviet Union taking pictures and flying too high to be hit by ground missiles, and then return in time to have a quiet evening helping their children doing their homework. Their wives thought they spent another boring day at the office.

Vintage Tri-motor at the Pima Air Museum

It wasn't a long day, and I arrived at the Cactus Gardens Mobile Home Community by three-o'clock where I indulged eating free soft ice cream in their community center. Bubba sure knew how to pamper us pedalers.

The following day we would be headed for a long day of climbing up to a high plateau where we would stay at our first hotel of the trip in the historic town of Tombstone. Before dinner we would get to witness a "shootout" in the tradition of the old west, and we'd been warned not to dither along the route as busses left sharply at four-thirty from the hotel. As it turned out, I wished I'd dithered.

Roadside pickup today was a **Purple Mesh Bag**

March 17 - Day 11

Tucson to Tombstone
73 Miles

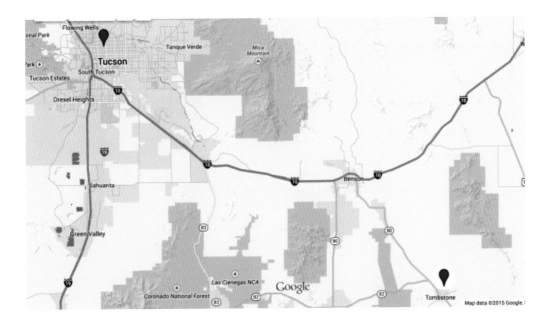

The breakfast schedule was moved up from seven to six-thirty to give everyone an early start toward Tombstone. The ride wasn't that far, "only" seventy-three miles, but there was a long climb through the Santa Rita Mountain Range that would slow many riders down. The need for speed was necessitated by our group going to the "Shootout at the OK Corral" mentioned earlier. It started at five-o'clock so we all had to be in Tombstone by four-thirty to catch the shuttle.

The morning ride was another bicycle-friendly experience as the temperature was mild, the sun warm, and the winds calm. The long hill, though described as very hard, wasn't nearly as challenging as many hills in New Hampshire, and I enjoyed the extra stress on my leg muscles. Jeff was the strongest rider in the group, with the slim physique of a Tour-de-Francer, and could easily outpace the rest of us which he did while climbing up the Santa Rita. As I pedaled dutifully along, I heard this *click, click, click* behind me, and suddenly Jeff zoomed by going twice my speed, head down and legs smoothly powering through their stroke. He often rode with his wife, Lisa, but occasionally he would break off on his own and put his body through its accustomed paces. On this day, however, he outdid himself as shortly, after he passed me I saw him racing back down the mountain. He told me later he wanted to support Lisa on her climb up, so after he reached the summit he went back down to see how she was doing. He climbed the mountain twice that morning! What a guy.

There was a SAG stop set up for us at an overlook yielding an impressive vista of prosperous looking ranches in the valley below. I seem to be stronger on the hills than on the flat, a phenomenon that has perplexed me, however I always breathe a sigh of relief when I see a sign indicating a sharp downhill grade. The ride down that day was exhilarating and I threw my bike into high gear and pedaled as fast as my legs would go. I've heard cyclists can hit sixty miles per hour on downhill runs, but the best I've ever done is forty, and I really have no desire to go faster. Tom always outpaces me on the downhill runs so he is more daring than I. We are both aware a spill at that speed would be injurious if not fatal. Spills would be much more likely with any kind of gusting winds, so if there is any wind at all I'm never so courageous as to tempt my fate. We seniors don't heal that fast once injured.

Ahhhhhh!

Geronimo!!!!

The landscape slowly changed from the sandy low desert, with its Saguaro Cactus and tumbling tumbleweeds, to a higher desert of scrub brush, mesquite, and prickly pear cactus. I did see an occasional Saguaro, but all I saw looked as if they would rather be living somewhere else. Deserts seem to favor life with prickles: rattlesnake fangs, cactus spines, Goathead thorns, and the like. Goathead thorns are an interesting breed of vegetation called Tribulus Terrestris for the botanist. It's a weed whose thorns are so well known for their ability to cause havoc it goes by many names, including Bindii, Bullhead, Burra Gokharu, Caltrop, Cat's Head, Devil's Eyelashes, Devil's Thorn, Devil's Weed, Puncturevine, and Tackweed; these are all in addition to Goathead. It is quite capable of going right through a bicycle tire and causing a flat which it often does. We heard that on last year's ride one cyclist pulled seven thorns out of his tire while fixing the flat caused by the eighth. Lisa managed to step on one that went right through her shoe causing a wound that bled freely. Fortunately the group didn't run into too many Goatheads on this tour as most of our flats came from glass shards and retread wires.

Goathead Thorns

Once we cleared the Santa Rita Mountain Range we lost our sun to scattered clouds that dropped a bit of rain from time to time. Again the landscape changed from scrub brush to lush grass covered prairie where cattle ranged free. We passed many entrances to ranches with their cattle brands displayed prominently on wrought iron arches spanning gated entries. Free range cattle doesn't seem like such a good idea to me as hitting a 2,000 pound steer at seventy mph with a semi might make quite a mess of the steer. On the other hand hitting one at seventy with a VW Beetle... Yuck! Fences are costly, so I suppose ranchers have done cost-benefit analyses and considered the risks worth it. On occasion we cyclists will encounter cattle guards, which are breaks in the pavement. These consist of steel pipes or train rails spaced roughly four inches apart at right angles to the direction of traffic, the spacing is just enough to catch the hoof of a steer and discourage it from trying to cross. Unfortunately the spacing of the rails is just enough to catch a skinny bicycle tire so one has to be careful to cross the guards at right angles.

The Good Old Days

Seeing "Open Range" signs perked up my senses to the possibility of seeing actual cowboys actually herding steers around the actual prairie just like in the old days. I thought I had one spotted when I spied a cowpoke herding a cow and her calf along a grass covered ridge. The cowpoke looked like he'd been up all night herding his two charges, as he seemed to be asleep in the saddle. He also seemed to be moving awfully slowly, leading me to believe he really had nowhere special he was herding them. My

Git Along Little Doggie

thrill wore off as I approached and realized these were artsy profiles stuck on the ridge to confuse and confound innocent passersby who longed for the thrill of experiencing the life of the old west. Somebody with a cutting torch and a pile of steel plate had made these profiles and mounted them on a ridge alongside the highway. I can't imagine a bored rancher doing anything like this, so I suppose it was part of an Arizona Tourist Board program, for which the rancher probably receives a nice monthly rent check.

Arizona Wine?

I was surprised by signs advertising wine tastings at local vineyards, never imagining wine was produced in Arizona. Actually, I didn't think wine was produced much at all in the south, but I discovered, thanks to Google when I returned home, that every state in the union produces wine. Wow, I never suspected that. Arizona, produces 0.024% of total USA production. That isn't a great deal, and it's possible Charron Vineyards produces the whole 0.024%. Just to round out the picture, California produces 89% of the total, Washington and New York 3% apiece, and the rest of the country the remaining 5%. Texas is the fourth largest producer, capturing its spot in the annals of USA wine GDP with 0.18%, honestly, 0.18%. I think they sell more than that in my local grocery, so I'm not sure it's a statistic of which Texas should be particularly proud. We have a vineyard near where I live in New Hampshire, the Mountain View Winery, but, sad to say, production is so low that it wasn't even mentioned as a contributor to total USA production in the list of producers.

All day I never lost sight of mountains as I either passed through their valleys or saw them ringing the horizon. Many appeared to be rock climber's dreams, though I didn't see any signs of climbers.

Rock Climbers Paradise

Ranch House Restaurant

As I biked further south and east, the landscape changed again and the prairie dissipated into scrub brush with nary a bit of grass anywhere. The ranches disappeared as did the vineyards and cactus. The land looked inhospitable, though houses still dotted the countryside; they were isolated, lonely looking houses, miles from anywhere.

It would seem to me that life under such conditions would be desolate. However, as I turned onto Route 83, there stood The Ranch House Restaurant in Sonoita, a delightful place with western ambiance and good service. Clearly the people who worked there didn't think of their lives as desolate. If they did, they didn't show it, as they were as nice as they could be. From Sonoita there were but a few miles to go before reaching Tombstone, so I rested my aching muscles for as long as possible at The Ranch House, munching fries and sipping Cokes.

Everyone's heard of Tombstone, Arizona, famous for the "Gunfight at the OK Corral," but how many know how Tombstone got its name in the first place? It seems a scout named Ed Scheiffelin was staying at a camp in the area established for chasing down Apaches. He would spend his free time prospecting and was told by soldiers at the camp that the only rock he'd find in Arizona was his own tombstone. Well, Ed found silver, staked a claim on his find, and called the claim Tombstone, more or less thumbing his nose at his detractors. So, no, it wasn't because there were so many people killed in the region that all one saw everywhere was tombstones, though I must admit that version holds a certain rustic appeal. Once word got out silver had been discovered at the Tombstone claim, the settlement grew from a few hundred to over 14,000 in two years and the name of Tombstone stuck. Ed Scheiffelin became rich, and Tombstone became a bustling metropolis in 1890 boasting a bowling alley, four churches, an ice house, a school, two banks, three newspapers, and an ice cream parlor, along with 110 saloons, fourteen gambling halls, and numerous dancing halls and brothels. Within a few years, however, the mines ceased to produce, and the population rapidly dwindled to its present-day 1,300.

Three "H" Club

Contrary to popular belief, the gunfight took place outside Fly's Photographic Studio, not in the OK Corral. It took place on Wednesday, October 26, 1881, when the population of Tombstone was at its height. Nobody outside Tombstone had any inkling anything had even happened the day of the fight until an author, Stuart Lake, published a fictionalized biography entitled "Wyatt Earp, Frontier Marshall" in 1931, two years after Wyatt Earp's death. The killing that took place that day occurred when five cattle rustlers were apprehended by the town marshall, Virgil Earp, assistant marshall Morgan Earp, and two deputy marshals, Wyatt Earp and Doc Holliday. The Earps were all brothers. Two of the rustlers, Ike Clanton and Billy Claiborne, turned tail and ran off. The other three - Billy Clanton, Ike's brother, and Tom and Frank McLaury - hung around for the shootout and were shot dead; not, however, before they had wounded Virgil, Morgan, and Doc. Wyatt Earp was the only one who emerged unscathed. One might imagine scenes like this were so commonplace in the old west that they didn't receive much notice, though this one was written up in the local paper. Curiously enough, Ike Clanton, one of the rustlers who turned tail, sued the Earps for wrongful killing, claiming his brother and the McLaurys had their hands in the air when they were shot. It's possible once the three rustlers were injured after the first volley was discharged, they threw their guns down and their hands up. The three marshals, upset at being shot themselves, blasted them anyway. The Earps were later exonerated of any wrong doing.

Gunfight Skit

Everyone arrived in Tombstone in time to take a shower and meet the four-thirty deadline for the bus to the shootout show. As the bus meandered through the "old town", I was sad to see it was nothing more than a hyped up tourist trap. I don't know what I was expecting, but the town looked more like dilapidated Disneyland than a prosperous Arizona community. I must admit, I was eager to see the reenactment of the shootout and curious as to how the troupe would turn an historic, thirty-second, lead-ball-flying, free-for-all into an hour of tourist entertainment. Even though the skit was billed as the "Shootout at the OK Corral," it turned out to be no more than a hour of slapstick comedy that made light of shooting people to death for no reason at all. I've long said the secret to happiness is low expectations, and I often disappoint myself for not taking my own advice.

This being St. Patrick's Day, we had a dinner of corned beef and cabbage fixed by Anne and Serge served in the hotel lounge. Those in the group of Irish origin all wore some sort of green accessory. The zeal with which this tradition is practiced by those of Irish origin I've never made much effort to understand. I also never knew until this day that corned beef and cabbage was an Irish dish. I always thought it was a New England dish, but then I'd heard a lot of Irish settled in New England, so there you go!

After seventy-three miles, my body clamored for the clean sheets and soft mattress of a hotel bed, and I headed there as soon as dinner was over. Rain had started earlier in the evening and continued through the night.

Roadside pickup today was a **Red *Dubai Golf Club* Towel**

March 18 - Day 12

Tombstone to Douglas
50 Miles

Map data ©2015 Google

Landmark Lookout Lodge

The management of Landmark Lookout Lodge prepared our breakfast giving Anne and Serge the morning off. The eating area was designed for a few guests at a time and was too small to accommodate a famished horde of forty-four cyclists all at once, hence, we were encouraged to eat in shifts, the slower riders eating first to give them an earlier getaway and more time to leisurely make their way through the day. Nobody paid any attention to this encouragement, and we descended en masse politely elbowing our way through the throngs hovering around the steam table containing scrambled eggs, bacon, and bagels. The crush around the food was handled in light-hearted fashion with everyone making way for everyone else. We Coasters were really coming together in a spirit of camaraderie and deference to the needs and desires of others.

The psychiatrist Scott Peck wrote a book entitled *The Different Drum* where he outlined the various stages a group goes through before they reach "community," and he designed seminars where groups that were about the size of our C2C group experience the process. Typical groups go through four phases, beginning with everyone being very polite but putting on airs, much like what one might encounter at a company cocktail party. Pretty soon, the barriers break down, people express their true feelings, group chaos prevails, and finally the false fronts dissolve and individuals feel secure enough to expose their vulnerabilities. When this happens there is a sense of closeness felt among all members; a sense of respect for the difficulties we all face as humans on this Earth; and a knowledge each would do whatever was possible to help in the face of another's need. Having been to a Peck seminar, I knew what this sense of community felt like, so I was pleasantly surprised that we coasters had reached this stage early in our trek. I found it remarkable and Bubba did too, mentioning on several occasions what a close, considerate community we had forged together. One key was all of us having a common interest in cycling across the country and weathering the challenges that such a goal presented to each of us. We were in this together, and together we would see it through.

I traveled through the faux western kitsch of Tombstone this gray and cool Wednesday morning to begin my long and arduous trek up and over the Hauchuca Mountains. It had rained the previous evening and was spitting rain in the morning, so I had my rain gear on. The higher I climbed, the cooler it got, so the slicker served as a welcome wind break as well as a rain shield. A SAG stop was set

SAG Stop in Huachuca Mountains

up about halfway up the mountain giving us all a chance to rest for a moment. Following a brief respite and three bags of Lay's potato chips, I again put my head down and pedaled up and up and up. One of those most lovely of caution signs with the truck at a downward sloping angle met me at the summit, and I plunged with gusto down toward the town of Bisbee.

Through not Over

Before getting to Bisbee, the road passed through the only tunnel encountered on the ride. It's a good mood booster to know you'll be going through a mountain rather than over one, but going through this tunnel was spooky. There was little light, I didn't have a headlamp on my bicycle, and, while I had a flashing taillight, there was no shoulder, so I had to ride in the traffic lane hoping I'd be seen by any overtaking motorist. Adding to my concern was the rain slick road, as the road in the tunnel was covered in rainwater that ran down the hill through it. Any spill from tires sliding out from under could easily prove fatal in the face of oncoming or overtaking traffic. Fortunately, all us Coasters made it through without incident and emerged unscathed to take the turnoff to Bisbee, Arizona, one of the most delightful towns we visited on our entire trip.

All of these western towns have an interesting history, most of it rooted in either mining or rail transportation. Bisbee's history was rooted in mining. In 1877, a prospector by the name of George Warren first discovered silver in the Cochise County mountains. The prospector persona is an interesting study. Certainly prospectors are driven by the excitement of making a discovery, an excitement few ever achieve, but they must also be comfortable with a lonely and physically demanding existence. I'm sure they have great expectations of sublime happiness if they ever do strike it rich, but the relation between expectation and happiness is a tortured road as I've noted previously. I don't know if George was ever happy, but he sold his claim to one Ed Warren in 1880, who went on to raise $80,000 from Dewitt Bisbee to start production. The silver didn't last long, but lo and behold, in the process of mining the silver, the most concentrated deposit of copper ore ever found in America, was discovered. The mine was then dubbed the Copper Queen and sold to Phelps-Dodge in 1885.

Mining was a dangerous business and when the miners of the Copper Queen faced unacceptable working conditions, they unionized in 1917 and struck for better working conditions. Phelps-Dodge struck back and, with a privatized army of police, arrested 1000 miners and deported them to Hermanas, New Mexico. This was known as the Bisbee Deportation in the annals of American labor disputes. Phelps-Dodge then hired a new crew and continued operations. While early extraction of copper ore was focused on underground mine shafts, open pit mining methods were introduced during WWII and the underground methods at the Copper Queen were abandoned. The ore from the mine eventually gave out and it was shut down in 1975. Today it is a tourist attraction with visitors able to plunge deep underground to experience what a miner went through back in the "old days."

Copper Queen Open Pit Mine

The men who risked disease and death to build Bisbee were honored in 1935 by the citizens of the Warren Mining District who erected a statue dedicated to, *"Those Virile Men, the Copper Miners, whose contribution to the development of the wealth and lore of the state of Arizona has been magnificent."* The copper hunk in the photo is holding a hammer in his right hand and a chisel in his left. His head is held high with his gaze taking in a future no doubt filled with great expectations. I've never made an association with mining and virility before, so I suppose these Bisbee lads were special. After a hard day at the ore face, about all I'd lust for would be a hot shower and a cold six pack.

It is tribute to the tenacity of the human spirit that Bisbee exists at all today. Here was a prosperous community of 20,000 people in 1900, hailed as one of the most cultured cities in the US, when suddenly, in 1975, its sole means of income dried up. Yet it endured, and it is now a targeted tourist destination with visits to the mines, boutique hotels, and upscale deli restaurants. In addition to the tourists it also gained a reputation as a new age destination for hippies tired of Haight-Ashbury city life in the San Francisco Bay Area. Lost looking souls were evident wandering the sidewalks and strumming guitars for tips on the street corners. If Arizona ever legalizes pot, Bisbee will be the state's epicenter and probably make more money selling marijuana than it ever did selling copper ore. The term "High Desert" will achieve a whole new meaning.

Virile Copper Miner

We Coasters ate lunch at the High Desert Market and Cafe and many of us hung out there for several hours enjoying the first sunshine of the day. We had time to kill as we couldn't occupy our rooms at the Gadsden Hotel in Douglas until after three o'clock. The

High Desert Market Cafe

Cafe stood out as the only deli I'd ever visited where I had ordered what I wanted from the deli section with nobody keeping track of what it was. I took a drink from the cooler and a cookie from the counter and went outside to dine. When it came time to pay I went back to the cashier who asked me what I had ordered and charged me based on my memory. I'd never seen such trust anyplace before. They might find it necessary to tighten things up as their clientele ages and can't remember they ate.

From Bisbee, Tom, Linda, and I flew downhill past the open pit, which has to be a good 1,000 feet deep and half a mile or more across. The highway ran right through one of the ore faces, but the sides were all fenced in so that curious onlookers wouldn't fall to their deaths. It was downhill most of the way to Douglas, with rain threatening the whole while. The three of us missed the rain, but groups both in front of us and behind us really got hammered.

Douglas was founded by one James Douglas, a truly remarkable Canadian of Scotch descent who had three passions: theology, medicine, and geology. He practiced all three during his professional career, but eventually settled on geology. He, together with Thomas Hunt, invented and patented the "Hunt and Douglas" process for extracting copper from its ore. This process came to the attention of the Phelps-Dodge company, who had all the ore they could handle coming from the Copper Queen Mine, so they hired Douglas to set up a smelter outside Bisbee utilizing his patent. Douglas picked the first flat spot he came to east of the Huachuca Mountains, an old army base named "Camp San Bernardino" established to chase Apaches, and set up his smelters there. Not knowing if the "Hunt and Douglas" process would really work as intended, Phelps-Dodge offered Douglas either a small flat fee for his services or a percentage of copper production from his process. Douglas, apparently a man of supreme self confidence as well as monumental ego, chose the percentage deal and became fabulously wealthy. The city of Douglas thrived until the Copper Queen mine shut down in 1975 and is today a shadow of its former self.

Camp San Bernardino, as Douglas was called back then, was some kind of wild place back at the turn of the last century, so wild that the Governor of Arizona sent in a contingent of State Rangers to pacify it in 1902. Even when it became incorporated as Douglas in 1905, thanks to the construction of the copper smelters, word among the Rangers was that Tombstone couldn't hold a candle to Douglas for sheer, wanton lawlessness. Then, in the midst of this wanton lawlessness, somebody decided to build the luxurious Gadsden Hotel to European world standards. The Southern Pacific Railroad had been completed in 1881 and it was easy for settlers to move west. The ranchers now could move their beef to market cheaply by rail, rather than by the time-consuming and risky cattle drive; Phelps Dodge could move their copper ore out of Bisbee to local smelters; and settlers could move goods and services in by rail. The area boomed. Clearly it was time for a hotel, and clearly the economy was expanding in Douglas sufficiently to support a hotel the magnificence of the Gadsden; this, in a city that was, and still is, remote and far from a metropolitan center.

Gadsden Hotel Lobby

The hotel was indeed magnificent. The spacious main lobby was majestically set with a solid white Italian marble staircase and four soaring marble columns. An authentic Tiffany & Co. stained glass window extended forty-two feet across one wall of the massive mezzanine. An impressive oil painting by Audley Dean Nichols resided just below the Tiffany window. The hotel's vaulted stained glass skylights ran the full length of the lobby. Then, in 1927, the hotel burned down. However, it must have been a great success prior to the fire because in 1929 it was rebuilt with additional floors and a foundation capable of handling up to nine stories. The lobby was saved, so the signature feature of this extravagant venture introducing culture to the desert was able to carry on for another ninety years.

Upon arrival in Douglas, Tom, Linda, and I went immediately to a bicycle shop to purchase some needed supplies only to find it almost empty. The clerk was Latino and informed us that the store in Douglas was a simply a shipping point for bicycle parts headed for Mexico. He placed orders with suppliers all over the world and they shipped to the shop in Douglas. Apparently distribution in Mexico is haphazard at best, and the only way the bike store in Mexico could be assured of having inventory was to have parts sent to Douglas and then transshipped across the border in their own truck. He told us deliveries headed south once a week. As a result, we left with nothing we needed. The rain then hit us, and we were drenched by the time we made it the six blocks to the Gadsden Hotel to find our rooms and flop on our beds.

Once we coasters got settled in the hotel, the rain began in earnest and hit Douglas in torrents. This made it impossible for Anne to prepare our dinner from her chuckwagon, so Bubba turned to and somehow got the hotel manager to agree to feed sixty of us even though his restaurant was closed for the night. The manager called in his staff to work overtime, broke out food reserves from his larders, and served up a great meal of quesadillas for everyone. One of the servers had worked in the hotel for thirty years, and she entertained us after dinner with stories of all the ghosts that had been seen in the hotel. She even had her own ghost story of a lady who brushed by her in the coffee shop, sat down in a booth, and then suddenly disappeared. It was hard to take seriously, but these stories have been featured on TV programs specializing in spiritual visitations, so maybe they're true!

Curiously enough, I wrote in my journal that this was the hardest day of all so far, as the cold was penetrating, the wind was in our faces most of the day, and the climb up the Huachuca Mountains was the most challenging so far. And yet, when asked at the end of the trip which day was the most challenging, I remember it being the long uphill slog into the wind to the Santa Catalina State Park outside Tucson. I had completely forgotten the ride up the Huachuca Mountains as posing any sort of extraordinary challenge. How quickly we forget.

Roadside pickup this day was a **Woman's Pink Tennis Shoe**

March 19 - Day 13

Douglas AZ to Rodeo NM
50 Miles

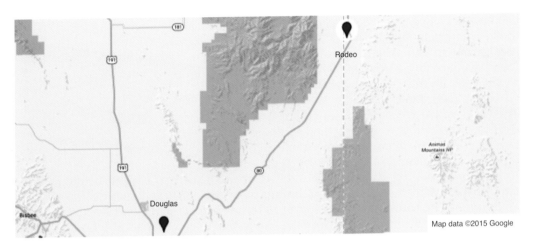

Map data ©2015 Google

The dawn of March 19 ushered in a cold and clammy mist, so I donned my warmest gear to face the ride to Rodeo, New Mexico. The forecast was for afternoon thundershowers, so most of the tour wanted to leave early to beat them to our stop for the night in Rodeo. Cold and clammy as it was, the wind was at our backs, and all things being equal, I'll take cold and clammy with a following wind to warm and sunny with a head wind any time. I buzzed along averaging about twenty miles per hour, a speed that didn't allow me to smell the roses, but it was just as well as there weren't any roses to smell anyway. What a desolate landscape it was from Douglas to Rodeo.

There weren't any places on this route where we could buy a sandwich, so Bubba arranged to have a sandwich spread set up for us at one of the SAG stops. This stop happened to be at the site where Geronimo surrendered in 1886 to U. S. Army General Miles. The Apache Tribe led by Geronimo spent years raiding cattle off the range, stealing horses, burning buildings, and killing noncombatants. The native Americans really had no chance of surviving against ranchers from the United States and ranchers from Mexico lining their governments up to send troops into the region. The fact they were able to hold out as long as they did is a testimony to their courage, determination, and resilience. The good people of Douglas erected a memorial to the surrender which "forever ended Indian warfare in the United States." It seems to me a more fitting tribute would lament the disappearance of a noble

Monument to Geronimo

way of life lived by a courageous, strong nation overwhelmed by events over which they had little recourse but to resist with all their strength.

Ever since entering Arizona at Yuma, we Coasters had been traveling through a part of America added to our territory by the Gadsden Purchase. This, as I had learned in junior high from Miss Marble, (and then promptly forgot) was purchased from Mexico in 1854 for the tidy sum of $10 million by James Gadsden, then America's Ambassador to Mexico. Traveling by bicycle puts one in intimate contact with the land one is traversing, and in doing so, I began to wonder about the circumstances of the purchase. Gadsden was a southern boy, a firm believer in the use of "African Domestics" to create wealth for superior white folk. He once advocated the separation of California between north and south so his favored labor force could contribute their services to the growth of the region's (and presumably his) economy. California rejected his plan, but it didn't deter Ambassador Gadsden from his dreams of territorial expansion. Being at one time president of the South Carolina Canal and Rail Company, Gadsden had many friends in the transportation sector advocating a southern transcontinental railroad corridor. As a result, Gadsden, when he was ambassador to Mexico, received permission from then President Pierce to secure additional land to clear the way for a southern route skirting the pesky Santa Rita Mountains. Gadsden's original proposal to then Mexico's President, Antonio Lopez de Ana, was for all land, including most of the current Mexican states of Baja California, Baja California Sur, Coahuila, Chihuahua, Sonora, Nuevo León, and Tamaulipas. The US Congress, however, fearing too great an expansion of territory favoring slavery, was opposed to this proposal. Santa Ana wasn't much in favor of the idea either, and so he and James Gadsden settled for a slice we were now traveling through until we reached Texas. Why Santa Ana settled at all is a tale we'll touch upon shortly when we bike cross Texas.

Gadsden Purchase*

Entering New Mexico

Somewhere along the route we passed into New Mexico, so Tom and I stopped to get our picture taken. On the approach to Rodeo (row-DAY-o), the state had installed an historic marker celebrating the completion of the Southern-Pacific rail link between El Paso and San Diego. When these railroads were built in the 19th century, there was very close cooperation between the government and the rail barons. The barons were given rights-of-way on government lands, and, since the U.S. Government owned all the Gadsden Purchase land from El Paso to Yuma, no negotiations among private parties and no confiscations by eminent domain were necessary by the barons. Cooperation between government and industry for the development of infrastructure seems currently out of favor, which is unfortunate because the whole country gains from state investment in transportation, communications, and agriculture.

In Rodeo, Tom and I stopped at the Chiricahua Desert Museum, which was stocked with beautiful silver and jade jewelry, many books on desert lore and animal life, and very little schlocky stuff. There was nothing, absolutely nothing, anywhere close to this shop, so the fact that it existed at all, let alone being a class act, came as a complete surprise.

Shortly thereafter, the two of us arrived at our site for the night, an estate, once owned by John McAfee, the software magnate who provided the world's PC owners with anti-virus software. He imagined this desert location would become *THE* go-to hang-gliding center in America, so he built a large southwestern style home with many guest rooms surrounded by several airplane hangers for his guest's gliders. He called it the Painted Pony Resort. McAfee reputedly spent over $11 million on the venture, but then ran into financial difficulty and had to sell it for ten percent of what he had in it. It is now rented out as a retreat and conference center, an ideal location for any organization that really wants to get away.

Rain began as a ripping thunderstorm in the early afternoon, and about half the Coasters arrived soaking wet. Unfortunately there weren't enough beds to accommodate everyone, so we drew straws to see who got a bed and who got an air mattress in a hanger. That being done, little by little everyone got settled into their assigned lodgings, stripped out of their wet clothes, took their showers, and lined up for dinner. March Madness basketball was being televised so an interested core group ate dinner off their laps in front of a wide screen TV. While devotees watched with earnest, those who could care less made wise cracks. Cecil, our celebrated soloist, serenaded us with "Ghost Riders in the Sky", a song I remember fondly from my childhood in Golden, Colorado. Everyone joined in the chorus, howling at the top of their lungs. This was truly a fun group with a vast range of interesting and congenial personalities.

We'd bunked on air mattresses in group settings before, so those who drew the short straws weren't too upset by the arrangements... until, that is, the next morning. It poured most of the night, and, it was discovered, the hangars leaked, so by morning a flood of water had soaked clothes, air mattresses, sleeping bags and inhabitants. After the rains, it turned cold, so not only were those who camped out in the hangars wet, they were exposed to temperatures in the high thirties. Bubba warned us the journey was to be an adventure, and it was a tribute to the positive mental attitudes of those who suffered through the night to view it as such. We, who were lucky enough to sleep in the main house, heard many descriptions but few complaints in the morning.

Roadside pickup today was a **A Plastic Doll's Leg**

*Map downloaded from internet

March 20 - Day 14

Rodeo to Columbus
95 Miles

Rain from the previous night produced a sea of mud in the dirt parking lot, a sea we all had to slog through to get to the breakfast tables Serge had set up. We prepared our oatmeal and bagels, and then slogged back to the warmth of the main house. It was a cold morning with the temperature dipping down to thirty-seven overnight, and I was in no hurry to hit the road until the air warmed up a bit. After breakfast I slogged back out to make a sandwich for lunch, as again there would be no restaurant along our ninety-five mile route that day to Columbus. The three mile dirt road between Highway 80 and the Painted Pony Resort was a swampland of mud, so, when it came time to depart, I opted to be driven to the main road in one of the SAG vehicles. Several EFIers (those who pledged to ride **Every F&%#ing I**nch of the 2909 miles and took their pledge

Painted Pony Resort in the C-O-L-D Morning

literally) chose to ride out through the mud but got bogged down and ended up carrying their bikes out. I was wearing all I had against the cold: full gloves, leggings, windbreaker, and ear warmers. The rain, however, had passed and the sun was out and the air clear. We all had a long day ahead of us, and I was hopeful the wind would be at our backs for much of the way.

The countryside between Rodeo and Columbus was stark and empty rangeland with endless vistas of scrub brush and sparse grass. There were signs for free-range cattle along the side of the road but few cattle to see. The signs seemed to harken back to times when the railroad was operational in the early 20th century and cattle roamed freely on the range until it was time for market. The railroad stopped working in 1954, but there was still a visible roadbed and dilapidated stockyards along the sidings for loading the cattle cars.

On and On and On and On

Nowadays we just fatten cattle up in pens. Alas, the legends of the cowboy are a fading figment of history. While on the subject of the cowboy, it is worthy to note that the term in the late 1800s was used to depict a lawless, vagrant who was as likely to rustle cattle as he was to drive them, downed whisky by the bottle, and murdered for the thrill of the sport. It was not a good sign if someone called you a cowboy back then. Of course many of the men who came west were veterans of the Civil War and used to a life of wanton slaughter and disregard for individual rights - a pretty messed up bunch if you ask me.

All Downhill from Here

Early in the ride as I was slowly going numb from the cold, I heard what sounded like geese off to the south. I looked to see what was about when a flock of about ten rose in their characteristic "V" formation, heading to the North. Soon, another ten rose and started circling about under the first. Both flocks were close to earth when the first V formation changed direction and started a turn around those below. Suddenly more geese rose off the desert floor, and more, and more until there were close to a hundred or so all swirling around each other flying higher and higher. When all the geese had taken flight, the ones at the top of the spiral in the "V" formation again headed North, and little by little, as all the rest reached the agreed upon elevation, they formed their own "V" formations and followed the leaders. It was quite an amazing sight.

This is the day all us Coasters crossed the Continental Divide, west of which all rivers flow west and east of which all rivers flow east. The divide in southern New Mexico didn't amount to much, even though it was close to a mile high, because we had all climbed this mile gradually over the past few days. By comparison, the Continental Divide in Colorado at Independence Pass is 12,095 feet, a steep climb going up and a steep descent coming down.

Along the way, the tour ran into an intrepid adventurer named Adam Bradley. He had biked to Alaska several times, biked across the country several times, and had a goal to hike up every mountain trail that bisected the US. He had done them all except the Sierra Trail up to Alaska. He was alone and carried everything he needed to camp out along his routes. He even had a satellite dish for blogging from isolated locations. Everything you see in the picture he carries on his back in the mountains. Yikes!

Adam Prepared for Anything

Hachita Stone Church

A luncheon SAG stop was set up at Hachita, a sad shell of a town that clearly had a history associated with the railroad. The crews for the trains lived along the route, and towns sprung up as bedroom communities to accommodate them. Here in Hachita I saw remnants of what was once a thriving township, including this unique stone church. Along the railroad bed stood a large, rusted out water tower, presumably used for replenishing the water used for steam locomotives. The advent of the diesel-electric locomotive made all these water towers obsolete, but many were still standing after seventy-five years of disuse. The tracks passing through Hachita all belonged to the El Paso & Southwestern Railroad, established by Phelps-Dodge to transport ore from the Copper Queen and other mines in the area to smelting locations. When the bottom fell out of the copper market following WWI, the EP & SW railroad line was abandoned.

All along the roadside between San Diego and St. Augustine I passed shrine after shrine erected to memorialize the victims of traffic accidents. Each of these was a reminder of how tragedy can strike without warning and often in the most unexpected places, like here in the desert. It just seemed impossible that a fatal accident could happen in an area where there is such clear visibility to oncoming traffic and so many opportunities to strike out across the desert if an errant driver strayed from his lane.

Descanse en Paz

As I came upon these grim reminders I thought it would be interesting to create a picture book of all the shrines along our route. There were dozens of them. I took pictures of the most elaborate ones, but there were so many that I didn't stop for them all. I am, however, perplexed by the motivation to erect such a shrine in the first place. They existed everywhere across this great land to commemorate the place of death, but it made more sense to me to erect a shrine over the remains of the deceased, not the site where they died. Maybe I'm just old fashioned?

The miles seemed to pass more and more slowly as time wore on. Not only did I think weird thoughts about why people erect shrines and what might lie under them, but my

Columbus Elementary School Gym

legs burned, my crotch screamed, and small hills seemed like major obstacles. I made it to the Columbus Elementary School in nine hours, arriving about the middle of the pack. The last rider finally made it in at seven pm to a standing ovation from the rest of the troupe. That night we bunked in the school gymnasium, but it was a night of fitful sleep for me as I had seldom before ridden so many miles on a bicycle. I downed a few more Advil than I probably should have to ease the pain from my aching body.

Columbus, New Mexico is famous, and the next day during our day off we would steep ourselves in its unique history and ultimate contribution to US preparedness for WWI.

Roadside pickup this day was an **Open End Wrench**

March 21 - Day 15

Columbus
Rest Day

This was a rest day in a spot in the New Mexican desert that I certainly never had heard about before we landed here. It's flat in every direction, windy, dusty, and hot, yet it has a fascinating history linked closely to Mexico and the wars defining the border between our two countries. Columbus Elementary, where we spent the night, was a brand new facility with 441 students, ninety percent of whom were native Spanish speakers. All the teachers were required to be bilingual and all students were encouraged to become fluent in both languages. With all the furor over "illegals" entering the US, it came as a complete surprise to me to hear that students from both Mexicali and Puerto Palomas were eligible to attend US schools and were bussed to and from their homes in Mexico each day.

Our first group visit this rest day morning was to the Pancho Villa Museum at the Pancho Villa State Park, the only state park in the nation to be named after someone who invaded the US. I had heard of Pancho Villa, nee Jose Doroteo Arango Arámbula, but I can't say I ever knew what he was all about. His beginnings were humble, but he was a man of great pride and national vision. His pride got him into trouble at an early age when he killed a man who had raped his sister, and then he had to escape to the Sierra Madre Occidental mountains to avoid prosecution. There, he teamed up with a Ignacio Parra, one of the most feared bandits in Durango. Between 1900 and 1910, he oscillated between the life of an outlaw, raiding haciendas, and a life of a Robin Hood, giving his spoils to poor peasants. Slowly, he gained a reputation as a daring adventurer with a noble heart, changing his name to Francisco "Pancho" Villa, in

Pancho Villa

honor of his grandfather, Jesus Villa. He was also known during that era as La Cucuracha, the cockroach in Spanish.

In 1910, Mexico was ruled by a dictator, Porfirio Diaz, and pressure was building in the country for a revolution to oust him. Fransisco Madero, a politician, convinced Villa he should devote his raiding skills to the ouster of Diaz and join the revolutionary army. This he did, distinguishing himself in several battles, most notably the one at Ciudad Juarez which he won. One thing led to another, and after several Mexican presidents had come and gone (most assassinated), U.S. President Wilson backed Villa to be the next president of Mexico. That backing lasted until Villa lost a battle to Venustiano Carranza, another candidate for president, and Wilson jumped ship to back Carranza as the next Mexican president. This betrayal didn't sit well with the recently defeated, now broke, and humiliated Pancho Villa.

All of which brings us to Columbus. Taking into consideration the fact that Villa needed money, that he was used to taking what he needed from his banditry days, and that he was thoroughly ripped at President Wilson for abandoning him, it stands to reason he might have looked at the bustling commercial center of Columbus, New Mexico as easy pickings for rebuilding his forces and getting even with America. In addition, it was rumored that the Ravel Brothers Mercantile, a general store in Columbus, had been paid $2500 by Villa for military supplies they never delivered, and Villa was simply taking back what was his due. On March 9, 1916, a force of 400 Villistas raided Columbus burning buildings, stealing anything of any value, and indiscriminately killing innocents. Fortunately for Columbus, there was a contingent of U. S. Calvary stationed at Ft. Furlong close to Columbus, and, equipped with machine guns, they soon had the Villistas on the run. On the American side eight soldiers and ten civilians were killed by Villa's forces, but the Mexicans suffered upwards of 170 killed thanks to the effectiveness of the machine gun fire brought to bear by the 13th Calvary Regiment.

Uncle Sam Wants YOU

This attack on US soil by a foreign power spurred Woodrow Wilson to commission General Pershing to go after him with the US Army. Pershing recruited an army to chase Villa down, never found him, but in the process Pershing developed the fighting force that would eventually become the American Expeditionary Force in Europe during WWI. This all took place in 1916. President Carranza was eventually assassinated by Obregon, his favorite general, who himself became president, and who, himself, was subsequently assassinated. Being ambitious in Mexico back then was a risky business.

Villa, well, he returned to his Bandido ways, but eventually agreed to stop his raiding and in return was provided an estate where he lived and housed 200 loyal soldiers, remnants of his diminished army. Then, on a routine trip to town in 1923, he was gunned down by seven riflemen reputedly commissioned by one of Villa's generals, Jesus Herrara, who had turned against him and supported Carranza.

We learned all this from a presentation given at the park in Columbus, The Pancho Villa State Park; a park named in honor of the man who burned the town to the ground, murdered ten of its citizens, and looted everything that wasn't nailed down. Some things are tough to figure.

All of us Coasters then went from the park down the street to the border with Mexico, where we crossed through our infamous fence into the town of Puerto Palomas. Here we visited a curio shop and restaurant called The Pink Store. It was packed with all manner of Mexican handicrafts, and most everyone bought something as a memento of

Por Favor, Señor

the day. The food was excellent and all who wanted one was given a free margarita with the purchase of lunch. Everyone was also presented with a souvenir ceramic cup on a ribbon to hang around our necks, perhaps with the idea we would buy shots of tequila to fill it. During lunch, a Mexican trio earned a year's salary in tips serenading us while an efficient wait staff served up mammoth Tex-Mex burritos, and everyone took photos of everything.

And Stay Out!

After lunch we wandered out to the town square, where a host of beautifully dressed children pleaded with us for the souvenir cups we had around our necks. Few of us resisted giving them up knowing they would serve little purpose back home and probably just wind up lost in an attic somewhere. We all figured it wouldn't be long before these same cups would be for sale to the unsuspecting Gringo

Ride 'em Pancho

who had just crossed into town and hadn't yet discovered the Pink Store and the free cups.

After assembling for a group photo in front of an enormous statue of Pancho Villa in howling attack mode located in the square, most of us wandered back across the border, climbed into the SAG wagons, and were deposited back at the Columbus Elementary School, where nap time awaited us on air mattresses, all thoughtfully inflated for us by the Wolfpack.

Wolfpack: Adam, Zach, Peach Fuzz, Chester, and Cyrano

One of the pampered features of the C2C was all the support we received by the staff who accompanied us on the trip. Many of the staff were volunteer, but there were five who did all the set up and tear down of the various overnight options, and these five were fully employed contributors. They were a fun bunch of congenial guys who Bubba labeled the "Wolfpack," and they did a terrific job loading and unloading gear from the trucks, setting up the tents at the campsites, and blowing up air mattresses. They went with us to Puerto Palomas during our rest day in Columbus and all wound up buying cowboy hats and ponchos. I think every cyclist with a camera took a picture of them hamming it up in The Pink Store.

While this was a rest day, my legs were still really sore and I couldn't wait to turn in. The following night we would be housed in a hotel where I could immerse my tired muscles in a hot bath and sleep in a comfortable bed that wouldn't go flat in the middle of the night.

Little things take on a whole new meaning when they are denied.

March 22 - Day 16

Columbus NM to El Paso TX
77 Miles

I spent a fitful night, and, as dawn cracked over the Sonoran Desert, my tired muscles let me know, Advil notwithstanding, they weren't responding as expected to the day of rest. Well that was just too bad for them. My aching body might have been due to my air mattress going flat in the night. The Wolfpack had provided a pile of extra blown-up mattresses for those of us so stricken in the wee hours, but I wasn't awake enough to crawl out of my warm, cozy covers to find the pile of full mattresses and drag one over to my spot on the gym floor. Nevertheless, with a body still in revolt and the dawn cracking I was ready to make eastward progress toward our quest. I had seventy miles to do this day, and I had pledged long ago to be an EFIer and do what needed to be done to plant my front tire in the Atlantic after pedaling every EFI. It was cool, forty-seven degrees, but with the sun rising and the wind at my back, I didn't dress as fully as the morning I left Rodeo.

More and more, people are getting interested in cycling, and one of the questions I'm continuously asked is how difficult is it to ride in a group. Newcomers to the activity might have seen video footage of the Tour-de-France with a huge string of riders all bunched up riding wheel to wheel in what is known in French as a peloton (Linda joked that "Pedafile" might be a better term for the bunch of riders). Of course, every now and then one of the riders takes a spill, and then twenty or more go down on top of each other with water bottles, elbows, and curses flying. Rarely do they all get up and those that do are often covered in blood. Hence the question, "Isn't it dangerous to go on a group ride?" The answer is, "No," since only experienced riders ever try peloton riding and in most group rides every cyclist goes at his or her own pace, and the group spreads out over many miles.

Why then ride in a peloton? Why indeed? Peloton riding is done to reduce wind resistance. The rider in front breaks the wind, and the riders following all take advantage of the vacuum caused by the leader. This is the same principle the geese use when they fly in "V" formations. In order to take advantage of the vacuum of the lead rider, following riders must ride very close to each other, and the closer they ride the greater is the chance of running into each other. Since the lead rider has the most work to do, the lead in peloton riding is continuously changing - the one in front dropping back and the second in line moving to the front. It is estimated that as much as thirty percent reduction in energy is expended by following riders over lead riders. Lead riders set the pace and it is a heavy responsibility to set a pace everyone can follow; too fast and slower riders fall out of the peloton, too slow and following riders get frustrated with you and don't want you to lead. The lure of peloton riding is the thrill one receives by participating with others of like mind and abilities, and the boost one gets from reduced wind resistance.

However, it is very difficult to ride in a peloton. Wheels, front to back, are only inches apart and, if they touch, the cyclist on the trailing bicycle is likely the one to go down. Wheels are most likely to touch when the front wheel of a trailing rider overlaps with the wheel of a leading rider by more than a few inches, and either of them makes a slight course change. Staying on course requires constant vigilance on the part of the following riders, vigilance that precludes relaxing and enjoying the scenery. Since most group rides are billed as good ways to enjoy the scenery, few tours, especially those targeted toward seniors, advocate peloton riding. Experienced riders have to choose between the thrill of the peloton or the enjoyment of scenery. Several of the cyclists on our tour had sufficient experience to enjoy peloton riding, and it was inspiring to see groups of three or four of them all moving cohesively as if connected together with bungie cords.

For those of you who have stayed awake nights trying to visualize what there is between Columbus and El Paso, I can assure you there is N-O-T-H-I-N-G. The desert just goes

Bull Resting Under a Tree

and goes and goes, with the road reeling off mile after mile in what is almost a continuous straight line. There is little to do but plug ahead and play games with your mind about how soon you'll see the next roadside mile marker. The miles ticked off in rather short order, as there was a steady tail wind, and I averaged about twenty miles an hour over a smooth road with virtually no traffic. It was certainly the easiest day of riding I had experienced to date, though the mileage was significant. It was a perfect day for peloton riding if that was your thing.

At one point in the desolation of the prairie, I came upon a bucolic image of "Ferdinand zee Bool" under a tree. There were very few cattle to be seen along the route, so this particular critter really stood out against the barren landscape. Not too far away, a calf wandered aimlessly along looking for something, anything to eat, so I presumed there was a cow somewhere, but I didn't see her. There were also any number of cairns positioned along the roadside, and I wondered what curious event could possibly have motivated someone to take the time to construct them. In addition to the numerous cairns, there were numerous Border Patrol trucks creeping along beside the road, their occupants searching for signs of human passage. Some were dragging gigantic truck tires alongside the roadbed to smooth out the surface next to a barbed wire fence so footprints of undocumented persons climbing the fence could be more easily spotted. At one point we saw two four-wheel ATVs painted in camouflage being driven by agents, also in camouflage, presumably chasing down signs of Mexican intruders. Several times we saw signs where ATVs had spun donuts in the earthen roadbed. All work and no play makes jack a dull boy, and, I can assure you, if I had a job as dull as catching renegades, I'd be looking for anything to keep me from going in insane. Spin a donut? You got it chief!

One of Many Cairns

Our approach to El Paso took us though the New Mexico suburb of Santa Teresa and by the Santa Teresa high school. They had emblazoned on their stadium the inscription "Home of the Desert Warriors," which I misinterpreted as "Home of the Dessert Warriors." Needless to say, I had never been able to remember how to spell either one from seventh grade onward, and I had this sudden amusing image of football players entering a stadium on a birthday cake float wearing helmets emblazoned with pictures of birthday candles. I then got to thinking about the trend in our culture to name teams after ferocious animals, and what it might take to change the paradigm and start naming teams after vegetables, milk products, and articles of clothing. The Yuma Yoghurts has a certain poetic ring to it, don't you agree?

Sunland Park, New Mexico, distinguished by its mammoth statue of Christ the King on Sierra de Christo Rey, lay to the west of El Paso. The statue was commissioned in 1938 by Father Lourdes Costa and carved by Ubici Soler, the same sculptor who did the Christ of the Andes in Rio de Janero, Brazil. Needless to say (I will anyway), the statue in Sunland Park bears a striking resemblance to the Christ of the Andes. Hikers up to the cross are cautioned to be wary of assailants intent upon separating them from their valuables - not a particularly comforting message demonstrating the efficacy of the statue's protective powers.

If You Can Read This I'll Be Yours

Tom, Linda, and I made it into El Paso in the early afternoon after crossing the Rio Grande, which was more like a sodden stream bed than a large river. The inscription in the sand read, "WILL YOU BE MY VALENTINE AN." Whether the author didn't know how to spell his girl friend's name or whether it was his initials is anybody's guess. Fortunately, he wrote his billet doux in sand in case he changed his mind, secure in the knowledge that his message would be erased after the next heavy rain. It seemed as I stood on the bridge a more appropriate name for the river would be the "Rio Nada," as there was almost no water in it.

It was my intent when I started out in CA to take a photo at each state line, but for some reason I missed the welcome sign crossing into Arizona. I'd heard they were having budget problems in the state and figured they probably didn't have the resources to put up a welcome sign. Then too, I thought maybe the state didn't really want to welcome anybody. The Arizonians certainly don't welcome Latinos, so perhaps they just pulled the welcome mat on everyone. I found out later that indeed there was a sign welcoming everyone to Arizona, but it was in the median strip and I was looking on the shoulder for it. My apologies

The Foor-Hawkes Trio

to Arizona for thinking I might not be welcome there. Jeff and Lisa Arndt came to my rescue and loaned me the picture they took.

El Paso had the first good bike shop since leaving CA, and Linda and I went straight to the shop to stock up on spare tires, tubes, pumps, chamois cream, gloves and other miscellaneous cycling paraphernalia. We Coasters were bivouacked in a hotel, and I certainly looked forward to a good night's sleep resulting in a body would be ready to go the next day. It would be a short day, only fifty-seven miles, but empty and desolate. Maybe there would be another tailwind. Maybe I'd see another "Bool."

Roadside pickup of the day was a **Snowflake Xmas Ornament**

March 23 - Day 17

El Paso to Fort Hancock
57 Miles

Entering El Paso from the west took us Coasters through the industrial sector of town, but El Paso is also an upscale University town hosting the University of Texas at El Paso, and the ride out to the East through the suburbs was pure delight. The day dawned warm, dry, and calm as we all threaded our way down quiet streets, modern houses, and well kept lawns in the hills before we dropped down and out through what was a booming, cosmopolitan center. Our route through the city wasn't too well understood from our route maps, so many of us cyclists simply followed our own instincts and turned down streets that seemed to take us more or less in the right direction. It was always a hoot to look down at a street crossing and see a small group of Bubba's Pampered Pedalers heading in the same direction on a different road of their choice. Eventually we all did converge on Route 2 heading for Fort Hancock.

Greater El Paso

Panaderia Tortilleria

Our first SAG stop was at a Latino market, the Panaderia Tortilleria, that has few parallels anywhere in urban America. The market held a vast bakery, restaurant, and a fresh vegetable selection the size of which I've never seen equalled in any American supermarket outside the Dekalb Farmers Market in Atlanta. There were, for example, a whole table of prickly pear leaves the Mexicans use as greens in salads, bins and bins of different types of chilis, and a food court specializing in fresh fruit and Mexican dishes. Virtually all the staff was Latino, and we were asked not to take pictures for reasons I can only imagine were related to documentation problems.

After leaving this stop we entered the countryside, which blossomed with endless agricultural fields. Pecan orchards went for miles as did acres of alfalfa and cotton. The land was crisscrossed with shallow canals that were fed with water pumped up from an aquifer by diesel-powered pumps. There didn't seem to be any effort to conserve water, as all the fields were irrigated by water-flooding, a process that California was trying to make illegal because it is so wasteful. It is really no wonder the Rio Grande has been reduced to a Rio Nada.

Pecan Orchard

Texas Apiary Outside El Paso

I was surprised by the presence of bee keepers and honey distribution centers. I stopped at one location to take a picture of the hives and first thing I knew, I had become a favorite of workers searching for new sources of nectar. Not that I'm not a sweet fella, but I didn't need a face full of bee stings with which to contend.

Lunch was at Margaritas, and I had the best Mexican pulled pork sandwich I think I've ever eaten - man-o-man was it ever tasty. As I sat eating lunch, two young women came in who were biking from Los Angeles to Boston, carrying all their gear and camping out along the way. What an adventure it was for them. Bubba invited them to stay with us in the Ft. Hancock High School Gym and share our table at dinner. He was very generous with fellow travelers, and it added a wonderful sense of community among all us two-wheel peripatetics.

Margaritas

The day was hot, and I wasn't fairing too well toward the end. My bike seat got awfully hard after a while, and no amount of "chamois butter" seemed to make much difference. I spent a lot of the ride standing up pedaling. It was such a relief to finally get into town and see the Fort Hancock post office. It was commissioned in 1886 when the town was renamed in honor of Winfield Scott Hancock, a Union Army General wounded at the battle of Gettysburg. Since Texas was a secessionist state during the war, it seemed a bit of a victor's poke-in-the-eye to name a town in Texas after an enemy's hero. In any event, the name stuck.

Fort Hancock Post Office

The town prospered for a while, as it was right on the main Southern Pacific railroad line, but it suffered decline, as did all the towns along the line, when the Southern Pacific ceased operations. Today about 1,700 people live in Fort Hancock and, fortunately for us, they had a relatively new high school where we Coasters bunked down in the gym. It seemed unusual for a school with only 179 students to have such a modern facility, but it is a tribute to Texans that they take education so seriously. Of the 179 students, we learned that almost all are Latinos, speak Spanish at home, and have relatives living just across the border in the sister city of El Porvenir. According to an ABC special report by Terry Moran in 2011, Fort Hancock used to have excellent relations with Mexico, as citizens of both countries moved freely and easily across the border. While Terry's report, reproduced on Youtube, emphasized the changed climate from cordiality to one of daily drug-related killings, I saw no evidence of any cross border activity during our brief stay. Clearly the border has been tightened up since 2011, and I was thankful for that.

Deserted Buildings on Ft. Hancock Main Street

For all aficionados of the movie, *The Shawshank Redemption,* it will be recalled that both Tim Robbins and Morgan Freeman entered Mexico at Fort Hancock after getting out of Shawshank Prison.

Dinner was served in a chapel next to the school where one of our cyclists, Joe, a psychologist, led us through a meditation routine attended by a handful of interested parties. After becoming one with everything, we had dinner and listened to a talk by the two women Bubba had invited to stay with us in the gym. They were on a mission to raise awareness to the dangers of using conventional methods to deal with menstruation, e.g. Tampax and Kotex, which can cause toxic reactions in women. Apparently there are alternative natural methods that are not only more effective but are non-toxic. Exactly how these two ladies expected to deliver their missionary appeal by riding their bikes across America wasn't obvious, and frankly I was not sufficiently interested at the time to quiz them on the subject. I now wish I had paid closer attention and found out what they were all about, but the talk seemed more oriented toward women so I ducked out.

Dynamic Duo Crossing America

Lights went out in the gym at nine and I settled in for another night of cramping muscles, snoring roommates, and possible deflated air mattresses. Everyone had to be out of the gym the next morning in time for the Wolfpack to pack up all our gear before school started at eight, so we were hardly off our air mattresses in the morning before they disappeared into the Penske truck. Mine stayed inflated this night.

Roadside pickup for the day was a **Full Size Bath Towel**

March 24 - Day 18

Fort Hancock to Van Horn
72 Miles

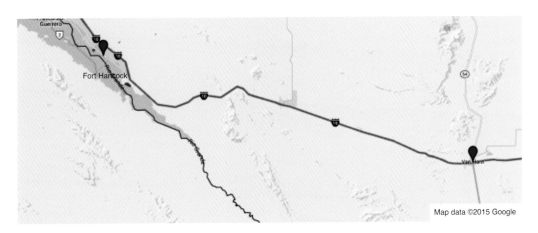

Map data ©2015 Google

It was cold, someone said it was thirty-seven degrees, but, even still, many of us were on the road before the sun was up. It felt good to bike along the back roads, passing freshly tilled fields and small farms with penned-in livestock as the sun slowly warmed the air. My fingers went from numb to workable in a few short hours. Again I was surprised by the number of bee hives clustered along the side of the road, as there seemed to be nothing in the way of nectar for miles in any direction. I also saw my first flock of sheep, not a critter I normally associate with present day Texas. I remember reading about the

Flock of Sheep?

prairie wars between the cattlemen and the sheep ranchers when the range was open and the animals roamed free. The sheep ate the grass down to nothing, so the cattle had no forage once the sheep had been through. Sure looks like a goat in the picture, though, doesn't it?

The day turned out to be glorious with a tailwind and ample sun. This was the second day in a row of cloudless skies, unlike last year when we were told there was a cold rain and nasty headwind on this leg. We also rode most of the day on Route 10, the old east-west road that had now become the frontage road for Interstate 10. Not only was well-paved, but almost empty of traffic. As the morning wore on, we began climbing into the Sierra Blanca range of mountains and in doing so encountered many signs of the dashed hopes and dreams represented by abandoned buildings. Miles from anywhere, I saw evidence of what looked like what once was a

Holiday Inn. The sign was missing, but the brickwork holding the sign was still standing. In the background stood the empty shell of a building where weary travelers once stopped to spend the night. Further along, as I entered the town of Sierra Blanca for lunch, I ran into an abandoned gas station, and it finally dawned on me that the construction of Interstate 10 bypassed these businesses taking them

Abandoned Holiday Inn?

Used to Be

off the main route across Texas. I believe this happened to many of the towns bypassed by the Interstate Highway System, whose livelihood was dependent upon travelers stopping for provisions. Sierra Blanca was one such town, but it was close enough to the Interstate to have a Subway restaurant built into a shell station and a marvelous restaurant with a sign out front indicating it was Delfina's Mexican Restaurant. When I went inside, however, the menus all indicated it was Michael's, so it left me wondering if Delfina held the mortgage and Michael did the cooking. Regardless, the food was terrific.

As I started the slow eastward descent along Route 10 from Sierra Blanca to Van Horn, I passed a Border Patrol check point. It was a little hard to picture what might be achieved by checking what little traffic there was along Route 10 when the bulk of the traffic was cruising down Interstate 10 right alongside of me. I was left wondering such thoughts when we passed from Hudspeth County to Culberson County, where we left Mountain Time and moved our clocks ahead to Central Time.

I couldn't resist taking a picture of John, who looked like he was ripping up a road sign in a fit of pique. He rode a recumbent bike, and while all the rest of us are taking "butt breaks," he was taking "leg breaks". John was in great shape, and he could outpace just about everyone else on his machine. Somehow I don't think I'd feel very safe riding one.

John Stretching

Just before we Coasters entered Van Horn we came upon a talc factory. I had always known talc was a mineral, but this was the first time I'd ever seen an actual plant. After all the furor over asbestos, which is also a mineral, it's hard to believe that talc is all that

Talc Factory

benign. It's been used as baby powder for years, and I anticipate the day when the New England Journal of Medicine connects talc to Alzheimers or autism or some other long-term ailment. After passing the plant, we had a short uphill stint and then a five mile downhill whoosh into Van Horn, with a tail wind and great road surface. It was the most exciting run of the trip, as I raced into town hitting thirty miles an hour.

One endearing moment of the day was meeting a young couple who had rescued a puppy from along the road. The lady was a vet, and between the two of them, they agreed to take the dog back East, Louisiana I think, and find it a good home. They had strapped a plastic milk crate to the back of one of their bikes in which they placed this cute little fella. He seemed perfectly content to ride along with them, paws perched on the side of the crate. He was an adorable fellow and hid under one of the trailers at the SAG stop looking out at the world and trying to process what it was all about.

I couldn't wait to hit the Motel 6 after a challenging ride through the mountains, gentle ones, but still mountains that left my legs a bit wobbly. These I would treat with a hot bath and comfortable bed - two attributes of a motel well worth looking forward to.

What a cutie!

It is curious to me that I can remember most of the places we stopped for the night in exquisite detail, but I can't remember the Motel 6 in Van Horn at all. I'm sure if I saw a photo, it would snap into place pretty quickly, but as I sit here and write this nothing, absolutely nothing, pops to mind. Early what? Not a chance!!!

Roadside pickup today was a **Red Tail Light Reflector**

March 25 - day 19

Van Horn to Marfa
72 Miles

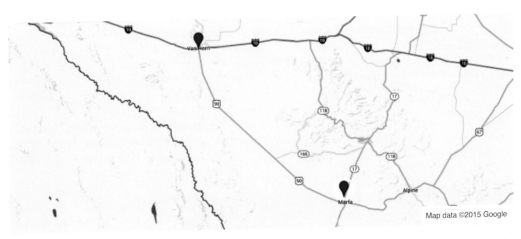

Map data ©2015 Google

Van Horn was an important stop for pioneers going west because of the Van Horn Well, an oasis in the prairie inhabited by Apaches, until Van Horn, a dutchman, "discovered" it and made a settlement there. Then the train came and the town of Van Horn became a permanent fixture in the west Texas plains. The Native Americans, well, they didn't cotton to the settlers and proceeded to raid the ranches springing up in the area. They endured the same fate as most Native Americans throughout the country, as they were hunted down and killed by the settlers and the army. The well water was artesian and came from an aquifer close to the surface, so locating the Southern Pacific in the area with its need for water to feed its steam locomotives made sense. As it turns out, the climate in Van Horn was heralded as being as perfect as it gets for the promotion of one's health, and one rancher, A.S. Goynes, once said, "This town is so healthy we had to

Woops!

shoot a man to start a cemetery." Curiously enough, legend had it he had said this before there was a cemetery, and he was later shot by his own brother-in-law. Thus he, himself, became the man who was shot to start a cemetery. You believe that?

In leaving Van Horn, our route took us off Route 10 and onto Highway 90, where my first experience was witnessing a semi-trailer that had tried to make a U-turn on a road with steep shoulders. The drive wheels of the truck cab lost traction on the shoulder and there the unit sat straddling the entire road and blocking traffic in both directions. One advantage to being on a bicycle was one's ability to slip around blockades like this and keep going.

As we left Van Horn we witnessed endless acres of cotton, alfalfa, and pecan orchards, all fed water by downhole pumps sucking from the aquifer. One pecan orchard went on for three miles with perfectly pruned trees all prepared to blossom for the next harvest season.

Chipseal Pavement

Traveling south on Route 90, I became painfully aware of a road surface called "chipseal." This is a paving technique used a great deal in the west, where a layer of oil is spread on an existing roadbed, and a thin layer of gravel is laid down on top of the oil. It is generally used on roads with light traffic where a strong surface isn't warranted. It's a very cost effective solution, but it has it's drawbacks including a very rough surface that causes vibration to all vehicles, particularly road bicycles that don't have any shock absorbers between the rider and the wheels. The rider is shaken mile after mile, and all the shaking takes its toll on one's energy level. It can take its toll on one's anatomy as well, as Gail chipped a tooth when her teeth chattered away on the road. All the vibration is also responsible for increased road noise from vehicles, particularly large trucks, and, while it is nice to be able to hear them coming from behind, the assault on one's ear drums is tiring. After a headwind, I rate chipseal as one of the most difficult riding conditions with which a distance cyclist has to contend, and I always breathed a great sigh of relief when I ran into a patch of smooth pavement. Curiously enough, road paving responsibility in Texas falls to the counties, and whenever we crossed a county line, we ran into different paving qualities. Most of the counties in west Texas embraced the efficacy of chipseal, but each had different specifications, which made crossing county lines an added point of interest, as we never knew what type of chipseal on which we'd be riding.

Texas Antelope

Cattle Roundup

And then the agriculture suddenly stopped and lush looking grass range surrounded us. Wayne was fortunate enough to witness a true cattle roundup with galloping cowboys herding steers through a fence into a new section of range. I'd been singing "Home on the Range" ever since I was a lad, but I don't believe I ever saw an antelope even in the years I lived in Colorado. But, there they were on the range between Van Horn and Marfa right in front of us.

Border Patrol Blimp

Off in the distance I spotted what looked like a blimp, which seemed a little out of place way out where where the buffalo used to roam. I didn't think blimps were used for much other than taking photos of golfers during PGA events, but there it was, on odd looking bird that seemed completely out of place. We later learned it belonged to our US Border Patrol, who would go up in it to search the countryside. They wouldn't get to see much except what was in their immediate range as the blimp was tethered, so all it could do was go up and down. It seemed to me our intrepid border patrol would be sitting ducks up there for anybody in a position to shoot the blimp full of holes. This was the only blimp of its kind we saw, so maybe it was an experiment that didn't prove too fruitful. Any intruder would certainly know they were being watched if the blimp was airborne, so they could just sit tight under camouflage until the thing was hauled back down. As I rode along, I began to think what would happen if the tether broke. I had images of helium filled balloons escaping from the hands of distraught children sailing off into space, each looking like a border patrol blimp. A cyclist will do anything to think of something besides chipseal rattling his brains out.

Around lunchtime, we Coasters reached Valentine, a community of 217 people with the town centerpiece being a picture postcard library. The library was the former home of one

Kay Johnson, a local rancher who spent her whole life in Valentine. She was a firm believer in the power of the pen, so the donation of her home to the community by her daughter, Karen, was a fitting tribute. The library sports floor-to-ceiling shelves filled with a varied assortment of reading material and quiet reading rooms for contemplation and study.

Four high school students had been commissioned by Bubba to make burritos for us, and they had tables set up in the yard behind the library where they were serving. Each had a dream to visit Europe, a dream that might seem a bit farfetched had not the senior class from the year before visited Italy. The dream was funded by charging two dollars for each burrito, which were so good most of us had two. As we sat around on the Astroturf munching our burritos and drinking chocolate milk, the superintendent of the school district came by to pay his respects. From him we learned that the entire school district has only thirty-seven students and that the four serving us that day were the only ones enrolled in the high school curriculum. These four were a bubbly, cheery bunch who clearly had solid, loving support from their parents and their community.

We were to see this time and again in Texas towns that might have seemed to move in the slow lane, but whose citizens appeared to have a solid grasp of what was most important in life. Tom and I donated an extra twenty dollars to the group's travel fund, so impressed were we with their positive attitude and willingness to work hard for the fulfillment of their dreams.

High School Seniors Serving Us Burritos

The Lady Loves Prada

After lunch, Tom and I headed back out to the chipseal pavement and a final run of thirty miles to Marfa. I had never heard of Marfa, Texas before, but apparently it was a rather well-known locale for those better informed than I about artsy communities. I got my first taste of the community's art orientation as we passed a project sponsored by two non-profits located in Marfa: The Art Production Fund, and Ballroom Marfa. Both seem to have been well enough funded to commission artists Elmgreen and Dragset, "to create something most unusual in the middle of the prairie." I'm sure nobody was disappointed. There in the middle of west Texas was a display stand filled with Prada products, products that never have had, and probably never will have, much future on the open range. The engineer in me, always seeking the best way to satisfy a need, can't seem to get his head around how anyone could come up with such a monument to impracticality. Maybe this project is a testament to the effects vast landscapes and hot sun have on the fragile brains of the human species. Go figure!

Bubba had warned us about a renegade deputy sheriff who took particular pleasure in pulling cyclists off the road with his flashing blue lights and telling them, for their own safety, Texas made it illegal for cyclists to ride on the road. According to him cyclists had to ride on the shoulder - even though it was often littered with glass, sand, pebbles, and cast-off truck retreads - all items making it far more dangerous than riding on the road. Actually, this fellow was dead wrong, and Texas law makes it very clear cyclists can ride on the roads, but must stay as close to the white sidelines as possible. He was very nice to me, and I thanked him for his lesson on Texas law and his concern for my safety. One

of our group, however, tried to tell the deputy he wasn't accurate in his interpretation of Texas law and was told he would have been arrested if it weren't for the fact the Marfa jail had no cell equipped for octogenarians. *Oooh!* For the following year it was suggested a quote from the Texas traffic statues be printed on our route sheets, so the 2016 C2Cers could politely read the law to the deputy and almost dare him to make arrests. Actually, it might have been kind of fun to get arrested and go before a

Not as Welcome as They Want Us to Believe

judge to expose the error of the deputy's ways. We'd probably just find out the judge was the deputy's uncle! Anyway, he didn't make any of us feel as welcome as the Marfa Chamber of Commerce advertised they wanted us to feel as we stood under their sign, being lectured by an authority figure who didn't know what he was talking about.

Presidio County Courthouse

Marfa was established in the 1880s as a railroad water stop and prospered as long as the railroad needed water. It was the county seat of Presidio County and was home to one of the more spectacular county courthouses in Texas. When the railroad's need for water dried up, Marfa fell into decline, but it had bounced back recently as an art center for minimalist art. The Prada exhibit certainly bears witness to a well supported minimalist art community in the area, minimalist in more ways than one. The town showed signs of decline, but there were also signs of a past splendor unmatched anywhere else in the old west. Besides the courthouse, which was built in 1886 and restored in 2001, was the Paisano Hotel with its elegant tile floors, antique fountains, and historic paintings hanging on every wall. Both were throwbacks to an era of rich cattle ranchers, railroad barons, and influential European architects. Marfa had also drawn the attention of Hollywood with the movie *Giant* starring James Dean and Elisabeth Taylor filmed in the city. More recently the academy award winning movies *No Country for Old Men* and *There Will Be Blood* were filmed there. On a stroll through town Tom and I visited a marvelous museum well stocked with artifacts and photos from the days when the railroad was king. Then,

Huh?

along our strolls, we stumbled upon another more eclectic museum, only open long after I'd planned to be sound asleep, offering a grilled cheese along with their collection of electronic wonders. Following our perambulations through town, we headed back to the Marfa Activity Center, a large gymnasium-like structure that didn't seem to be aligned with any school, church, or community center, where we bunked for the night.

Tired as we were, most of us elected after dinner to travel to a rest stop just outside Marfa to see if we would be lucky enough to witness the famous Marfa Lights. Actually, they weren't famous enough for me to have ever heard of them before, but they were a "must see" tourist attraction if one ever visits Marfa. The rest area was built as a viewing area with a veranda oriented toward the light source and enough parking for the inevitable wave of tour busses arriving each evening. Apparently the lights weren't visible every night, but I was lucky enough to see them this night. As I peered into the

Marfa Lights Viewing Center

dark outline of rolling hills, a white light appeared and began a meandering traverse down the mountainous silhouette. As it moved along, another appeared above it and began it's own path across the landscape. This scene repeated itself as more lights appeared, often two or three at once, all starting in different places, and all moving at different speeds. Some were very bright and some barely visible. Apparently the lights had been visible for centuries, as reported by ranchers, Apaches, and tourists alike. Sometimes they were red and sometimes blue, in addition to being the white I saw that night. What is most amazing about the lights is that nobody has figured out what they are, though there have been some attempts by scientists to do so. I suppose if anyone really wanted to find out what

The photo of the lights was taken from the website "Livescience".

they were, it wouldn't prove to be too difficult. But, since they are such a popular tourist attraction, who would want to mess with the mystery enough to pop the tourist bubble. I like the theory about wandering ghosts of Spanish conquistadores. I'm only surprised the art-focused Chamber of Commerce hasn't taken to promote the area through Marfa Lite beer and Marfa Lites cigarettes.

Roadside pickup today was a **Bouquet of Paper Poinsettias**

March 26 - Day 20

Marfa to Marathon
57 Miles

Map data ©2015 Google

We all awoke in the Marfa Activity Center to cold temperatures in the thirties, and I was blowing into my hands as I filed out to the breakfast buffet set up outside the center. This did not bode well for a comfortable day as I began the process of layering all the cycling clothing I had brought with me before venturing forth to face the challenges ahead. This day the challenges were temperature and wind with the addition of low oxygen levels at the mile-high elevation. In addition, we had some climbing to do for the first twenty-six miles. Off I went, my psyche steeled for what turned out to be a really nasty ride into our first SAG stop in Alpine, Texas.

First was the cold. I don't handle cold well as I have a condition called Raynaud's Syndrome where the blood in my hands and feet decides it would rather sit by the fire in my belly than venture forth to my extremities. My fingers and toes slowly grow white as the blood recedes, and then they go numb. The exasperating result of this condition is that it takes really elevated temperatures to dislodge my red corpuscles from their cozy seat by the fire and get them to venture back to my digital capillaries. I have often been unable to get the blood circulating without plunging my hands into a basin of the hottest water I could stand and then watch, transfixed, as my snow-white fingers slowly turned red. So, in spite of all my clothing, my hands were numb within the first five miles, and I couldn't feel the shift lever on my bike. Raynaud's is a precursor to frostbite, gangrene and amputation.

Great start!

Then as the morning progressed, it clouded over and the wind came up putting wind chill factors in the low thirties and high twenties. I was already freezing, so the wind chill didn't add much to my discomfort. The wind, however, didn't just blow steadily, but whipped around, gusting first from one direction, and then another. I mentioned before that gusting winds are disconcerting on a bicycle as there is something of a fine line between being balanced and upright and unbalanced and down on one's side. Not only did we have to contend with the natural gusting of the wind but also the gusting caused by passing semi-trailers. Semi's create a bow wave off their cabs, which is followed by a vacuum behind the initial wave. All cyclists riding on major roads have experienced this and made the necessary adjustments to their riding postures when they catch a glimpse of a semi in their rear-view mirrors. However, when the blast of the bow wave is accompanied by a gust of wind coming from an unexpected different direction, it can throw a cyclist's balance into the red zone. It's just no fun to ride scared, and this day I rode scared. Some Coasters chose to ride SAG vehicles into Alpine rather than ride cold and scared. Who could blame them?

Ghost Bike

There was one eerie sight along the highway of a pure white bicycle chained to the fence. There was just no telling what this was meant to signify, perhaps minimalist art, but it had the ghostly aspect of the crosses we'd encountered to mark the spots where unfortunate motorists were killed. Did this mark the spot where an unfortunate cyclist was killed? Maybe he had Raynaud's syndrome and his hands couldn't work his brakes. *No, No, don't think about it, just put your head down and pedal on.*

It took about four hours for me to climb the hills, and all I recall about those four hours was a grim determination to keep pedaling, keep pedaling, keep pedaling... through the wind, the cold, and spitting rain. At one point I passed a fellow cyclist changing a flat tire and remember thinking how there was no way I could have changed a tire with my frozen, dysfunctional hands. But, hey, I took the EFI pledge and plunged ahead in the spirit of the Light Brigade Charge.

The arrival in Alpine was a huge relief, and I headed immediately for the Bread and Breakfast Cafe where all forty-three of us (Roger left us in El Paso) descended like a plague of locusts, virtually cleaning them out of everything. I wrapped my hands around a large hot chocolate I didn't drink until it was too cool to

Defrosting Cyclists at the Bread and Breakfast

Marathon RV Park Cabin

promote any more circulation to my fingers, then I drank it and ordered another one. I think I was in the cafe for two hours or more, centering myself for the next surge into the unknown. Fortunately the weather lifted, the air warmed up, and by the time we hit the road again, the sun was out and a steady following wind ushered us along. By the time we reached the Marathon RV Park, where we were bivouacked for the night, the temperatures were in the sixties and there wasn't a cloud in the sky.

The park was beautifully laid out in a southwestern motif with private cabins, tent spaces, and parking pads for trailers and recreational vehicles. All us cyclists had tents for the night, but the staff was lucky enough to have the cabins, a treat they certainly earned for all the hard work it took to keep us Coasters pampered.

It addition, the park had a large outside patio furnished with tables and overhead propane heaters where vacationers could gather away from their cabins, tents, and trailers. Adjoining the patio was a well equipped kitchen, where Anne prepared our meals. The "snack" before dinner on this day was chile, and here we all are in the picture sitting around in the sun downing some of the best chile I'd ever eaten. Chile seems to be the perfect food to eat after recovering from a hard day of exercise in the cold. I know I always loved chile, even canned chile, after a day of skiing.

Marathon RV Park Patio

There must have been several railroad crossings in Marathon, as the trains coming through blew their whistles several times as they passed; and pass they did, at very high speeds. The first came through after we were all nestled snug in our beds, and Leapin' Lizards it made so much noise as it approached that it seemed to be cutting the campsite in half. After the first one, I kind of enjoyed the sound as it came at us in a high pitch and went away at a steadily lower pitch thanks to the Doppler effect. The enjoyment wore off after a while as I curled into a tighter and tighter ball to ward off the cold penetrating my tent like an uninvited and most unwelcome visitor. In the morning, all the tents were coated in frozen dew.

Roadside pickup for the day was a **Porno DVD Entitled** ***Chicks with Big Dicks***

March 27 - Day 21

Marathon
Rest Day at Big Bend

The propane heaters were especially welcome in the morning as many of us gathered in the patio waiting for breakfast stomping our feet and rubbing our hands under the warmth projecting from the overhead heat sources. With breakfast out of the way, those who chose to climbed into vans Bubba had rented for the thirty-nine mile drive to Big Bend National Park. Those who didn't go to the park took the rest day seriously and actually did rest their aching muscles lounging around the RV park.

Big Bend is a national park located on the Rio Grande, A.K.A "Rio Nada" by yours truly, where it makes a big bend through the Chisos Mountains. Actually there was a lot more water in the river going through Big Bend than there was in El Paso, so perhaps Rio Medio would have been more fitting. The park is larger than Rhode Island, encompasses huge tracks of the Chihuahua Desert, and is so remote it is only visited by 350,000 tourists a year, while other parks in the US attract millions. The river runs 118 miles down the southern boundary of Texas with Mexico, and, while it seems like it would be a prime entry point for illegal entry, apparently it is so mountainous and the desert so uninviting as to make it a very difficult and dangerous way to enter the US. Also, I'm

Wolfpack

beginning to get the idea that there are favorite routes for illegals to cross the border, known routes with known dangers, and that there are plenty of opportunities for alternative routes to be developed. Certainly, getting into Big Bend from Mexico would be easy - getting out maybe not so easy. All roads leading to the park have US Border Patrol Stations, and all vehicles are inspected, so any illegal getting into the park would have to get through it on foot. Our convoy of eight vehicles was inspected closely by trained dogs sniffing all around, sniffing, I strongly suspected, for marijuana, not undocumented cross-border travelers.

While on the subject of undocumented persons, it is interesting to note that helping Mexican citizens crossing into the US is not only against US law, it is very dangerous for the person so doing. Ranchers who have saved the lives of destitute desert travelers by offering food and water become known for their benevolence, and their homes become destinations for future travelers. If the future travelers are associated with the drug cartels, then denying them aide can make the ranchers targets for blackmail, or even death. Being a Good Samaritan has its down side.

During our journey to and from the park, we stopped frequently along the way to take pictures, take bathroom breaks, and spend money at visitor centers. The scenery was endlessly beautiful, with many of the wild flowers for which the high desert is famous in full bloom. Cactus flowers are some of the loveliest, and we were lucky enough to catch them after the rains. The huge white flowers topped with red tips of the Yucca were particularly impressive, but I think my favorite was the flower of the prickly pear. In addition, we saw a profusion of desert marigolds and bluebonnets along the road as we passed down to the first of several visitor centers. The visitor centers were modern oases of information, merchandise, and nourishment, but it was hard to feel totally comfortable with them as the prices seemed exorbitant - a necessity with visitor turnout so low.

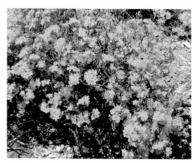

Yucca   Prickly Pear   Desert Marigold

From the visitor centers, we walked short distances to panoramic views of spectacular scenery and stunning rock formations. All this desert land was once a vast inland sea, and the formations were all cut by the action of waves against what was once shoreline. This activity produced such interesting formations as Mule Ear Peaks and Cerro Castellan.

Mule Ear Peaks   Cerro Castellan

Millions of years ago, as the inland sea receded, the Rio Grande River was a raging rapids managing to cut three deep gorges through the rock before settling on its current course. Curiously enough the river is called the Rio Grande (Spanish for "big river") by the US and El Rio Bravo del Norte ("fierce river of the north") by Mexico. It seems early in its history, when the entire region was inhabited by Spanish speakers, it was called Rio Bravo in the North and Rio Grande in the South, with settlers in the region not realizing it was the same river. Then in 1848, when the Treaty of Guadalupe Hidalgo was signed, text in the treaty read, "Rio Grande, otherwise called Rio Bravo del Norte." The US chose "Rio Grande" and Mexico chose "Rio Bravo del Norte." The Mexican contingent at the signing was probably still smarting from the loss of the war and didn't want to appear too compliant.

Gorge Cut By Rio Grande of Old

Kayakers Returning from Paddle Upriver

We stopped at one rest area down by the river, and several of the group took a hike up the Santa Elena Trail into one of the gorges cut by raging rapids of old. This particular spot is known as a convenient location to take a kayak up into the gorge, and we saw a couple of ladies who had made the trip in the morning and were returning just as we arrived. The water there was shallow, and our Wolfpack, seen sitting on the park sign above, went across to Mexico and had a great time joking about being "wetbacks" entering the US. Chester even had us all laughing at his characterization of an African having had to swim the Atlantic and trek all across Mexico just to get to America.

At another visitor center and ranger station, we learned of a vast cotton growing operation that existed along the river during the 1930s. Steam powered pumps irrigated the cotton fields from the Rio Grande, and at one time a steam powered cotton gin was installed to prepare the cotton for spinning. The enterprise folded in 1942, several years after the area was made a national park. In *Beneath the Window, Early Ranch Life in Big Bend Country*, Patricia Clothier tells of her life growing up on one of the hardscrabble ranches in Big Bend. It's a marvelous read about Patricia's extraordinary happiness as a child in Big Bend while her parents suffered day after day of back breaking hard work and endless disappointments.

Steam Powered Engine Used to Drive a Pump

It was a long haul back to Marathon, and though I had done almost nothing all day but sightsee, I was pretty tired, probably fatigue left over from the previous day. I made sure to wear plenty of clothes to bed, as I knew temperatures were going to drop and I wasn't disappointed. All I could think of was the joke about the Antarctic Kiki bird who went around chirping, "Ki, Ki, Ki, Ki, Ki, Christ it's cold down here."

March 28 - Day 22

Marathon to Sanderson
55 Miles

Map data ©2015 Google

We awoke to a morning less chilly then the previous one, but it was cold enough to be uncomfortable. I thought I had put on enough clothes before going to bed to stay warm, but I hadn't. It's funny that I could lie there knowing I was cold, but I couldn't muster the fortitude to get up, turn on a light, get out more socks and an additional long sleeve shirt. No, I just curled up into a tighter and tighter fetal position, fell back into a shallow sleep, and consumed the hours with weird dreams. As a Boy Scout I never liked camping much and still don't.

The day dawned about seven, breakfast was at eight, and the whole contingent of cyclists was on the road by nine. I hadn't had to put air in my tires in three weeks, an unusual situation that puffed up my ego and made me feel superior to all those on the trek who had experienced flat after flat after flat along the route. My head got really small really fast when, within the first five miles, I felt myself bouncing down the road. I was fortunate because the bike mechanic, Chandler, came along just as I was taking off my wheel, and he finished swapping out my tube for me. A shard of glass had gotten stuck in my tire and finally worked its way into the tube.

There was little but west Texas rangeland almost the whole fifty-five miles between Marathon and Sanderson, but I did pass some interesting knolls rising up out of the prairie. I wish I knew a definitive answer as to the origin of these geologic phenomena, but my sense is they are caused by igneous intrusions at a time when the area was experiencing intense volcanic activity. The intrusions of magma then solidified within the volcanic cone, which washed away when the land was enveloped by the inland sea covering the area. Who knows, but they do make for interesting speculation as I rode along with nothing else to think about. The day was an easy day with the SAG stops a good place to relax with comrades, and I hardly needed to pedal as the wind blew from behind the whole way.

SAG Stop on the Way to Sanderson

It appeared Sanderson was the Cactus Capital of Texas, fame the origin of which left me a little perplexed. I wondered what criteria exists that allows Sanderson to call itself the Cactus Capital, but then, I doubt there is much competition for the title, so probably nobody cares. I've always gotten capitol and capital spelling mixed up so of course my

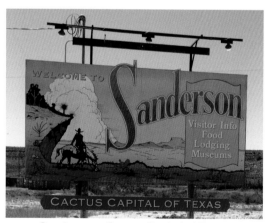

Sanderson - Cactus Capital of Texas

mind immediately started wondering if the good people of Sanderson used prickly pear leaves instead of the almighty dollar for their commerce. Sure Sam, anything you say!

There certainly isn't much in Sanderson, and the one mall I saw on the main road was up for sale. We Coasters were staying this night in the Sanderson High School gymnasium. I had been continuously impressed with the quality of Texas school facilities. All the small towns we'd been through had modern school facilities even though their student bodies were often quite small.

Once arriving in Sanderson and locating my kit in the gym, I wandered past the Terrell County Courthouse and over to the town library that had high speed internet. The population of Sanderson is less than 1000, but the library was relatively new with attributes like high speed WiFi that one might expect from a far larger community. Sanderson is a very close knit unit of concerned citizens motivated by a desire to lead simple lives and do as much good as they can with their time on mother Earth. The librarian had left Sanderson at an earlier time seeking fame and fortune in a more cosmopolitan setting. She later realized there was nothing of any substantive value in running

Terrell County Courthouse

the great American rat race, and returned to Sanderson to raise her family. Such people were evident supporting the entire senior class of six students who prepared our dinner for us as part of Project Graduation. Bubba is a retired police officer, and he told us that whenever he had been assigned the graduation beat, a teen was killed in a car accident that he had to go investigate. He was a firm supporter of Project Graduation as it had been very successful in preventing such needless loss of life.

Sanderson High Senior Class Minus One

The influence of concerned parents was evident throughout the meal as they hovered in the background supporting their sons and daughters, all of whom, by the way, had dreams to attend college and become all they were capable of becoming. All across Texas we just could not have found nicer youngsters anywhere in America.

After dinner, we were treated to an interesting talk given by a Captain Santiago Gonzales of the US. Border Patrol. Because of his Latino name, I thought he was naturalized Mexican, but he spoke English without any accent, so I began to wonder. His unit was responsible for eighty-two miles of border along the Rio Grande - a border so filled with mountains and steep canyons a fence was impossible. He indicated that they had apprehended up to three hundred people a month trying to make it to some destination in the states, but he guessed at least as many made it past them. The most interesting statistic was that of all those they apprehend, eighty-five percent of them, called "mules", are running drugs. Each mule carries a sixty-five pound bail of marijuana, and when approached by a border patrol agent, they all scatter. Each mule can make five hundred dollars for each bail they deliver to their ultimate destination. Many of the Mexicans are returned to Mexico when caught and immediately grab another bale and head back across the border. They can easily support a family for a month on one successful drug run, so for them, it's worth the risk. In one ironic twist, Agent Gonzales told us they now have a bigger problem with marijuana coming into Texas from Colorado than they do from Mexico. As the world turns, ain't it wonderful?

Following the talk, all who were interested visited the Border Patrol Headquarters in Sanderson - a building with bulletproof glass, cameras on every corner, four prisoner cells, and a control room filled with monitors. Captain Gonzales showed us pictures taken by their $150,000 infrared camera that can highlight bodies up to ten miles away at night in the desert. He was a decent fellow with a mild manner and quiet persevering way with words. He told us he gives each person he catches all the information they need to make an informed decision about what choices they have vis-a-vis immigration regulations. Since most are running drugs, those choices are limited, but, for those who are joining family, apparently there are choices besides immediate deportation. Linda asked if he felt any sympathy for those trying to reach family or for those whose families the authorities were breaking up, and he said he was just doing his job. Talk about irony, though - we found out his mother was an illegal immigrant from Mexico and raised him as a single mother in Chicago. My jaw dropped. Only in America!

On the grounds of the Border Patrol station we encountered what looked like a herd of twenty or more deer. They were just milling about and didn't seem particularly concerned about our presence. I had seen almost every pickup truck in Texas sporting a massive tubular steel grill, sort of in the spirit of early locomotive cow catchers, and, sure enough, Agent Gonzales said they were necessary for protecting the trucks when a deer is hit at seventy miles an hour, which apparently happens all the time. *Sheesh!*

To make the night interesting, somebody left the door to the gym open, and a skunk found its way among us. The smell was so strong where I was sleeping I was afraid I'd wake up with it curled up next to me. I then had a devil of a time getting back to sleep, plagued as I was by thoughts of skunk and all the various snoring sounds spewing up from mattress after mattress. I eventually did drift off, and by morning the smell was gone. Asking around, it seemed I was the only one who smelled it. Maybe I dreamed it. Could that have been possible?

Roadside pickup for the day was an **Award Medallion for Some Other Biking Event**

March 29 - Day 23

Sanderson to Comstock
82 Miles

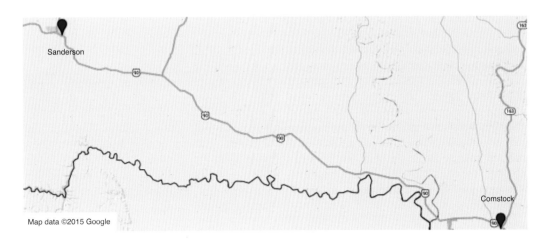

Map data ©2015 Google

March 29th was a Sunday, a day when school was not normally in session, but the senior class of six students were all up early to prepare breakfast for us. They then they stayed for our departure and all stood around cheering as we headed east. I was totally impressed with the kindness and consideration they demonstrated from such a remote location in west Texas.

House with Two Porticos Labeled "Mutt" and "Jeff"

Remote as Sanderson might have seemed to us, there were amusing signs of a community enjoying itself and the image it projected to the world. I went slightly out of my way to see a house built with two porticos, one labeled Mutt and the other Jeff. Who Mutt and Jeff might have been to the owner of this house was never revealed, but whoever it was went to a lot of trouble to make his statement. Maybe it was her statement? Who knows? I know I would have liked whoever owned the house.

It was a long slog this day, but more interesting than some coming before. There were signs everywhere of abandoned buildings, presumably reflective of the lost business when Highway 90 was bypassed by Interstate 10. I liked the one that had "Hello

Nothing" spray painted on its side. The day was made difficult due to a persistent headwind, and pedaling up the rolling hills on chipseal into the wind made the whole day tough.

Our designated lunch stop was in Langtry at a roadside store whose proprietor was a stone merchant as well as storekeeper. The tables and benches were massive chunks of what appeared to be limestone laid down when the area was a vast inland sea. At this same site last year, a cross country cyclist hobbled up to the restaurant with three missing spokes in a broken front wheel. He had stopped his journey there with a bike frame loaded down with all his camping gear and a front wheel that was hardly turning. Bubba just happened to be having lunch when this traveler staggered into the store, and, when Bubba inquired about

Hello Nothing

his plans, he said he was going to abandon his bike, load all his gear on his back, and hitchhike to the nearest town with a bike shop. Bubba didn't hesitate a minute, but called in the C2C mechanic who was well stocked with rims, spokes, and tires. Within an

Check Out Those Tables

hour, the traveler's bike was fixed and ready to go. If ever there was a story about serendipity, this has to be one of the best I've ever heard. To be broken down in a remote town in west Texas hundreds of miles from the nearest bike shop, only to run into the one person within those hundreds of miles who could help you, has to rate as some sort of miracle. It's also quite a testament to Bubba's generosity and one of the reasons his tours are so successful. He is just enormously well prepared for any contingency.

The town of Langtry was a short jaunt off Highway 90, but it was well worth a visit to the state museum celebrating the life of Judge Roy Bean. Phantly Roy Bean, Jr. was a character. As a young man he was a womanizer, often running afoul of men whose women he was ...izing. He killed one of the men and was caught and sentenced by those who caught him to hang by the neck until dead. Reputedly, he was hung by the neck sitting on a horse that didn't bolt when the executioners rode away. There he sat until he was saved by the wife of the man he had killed. Now if you believe that... but I digress. At

one time he ran a slaughterhouse that he kept supplied with rustled cattle. He went on to being a saloon keeper opening a saloon out of a tent in a railroad camp with 200 migrant workers. The camp was a wild place needing some justice, so Phantly Roy Bean, Jr. was selected to be the Justice of the Peace. Why a saloon keeper with a felonious past without any legal

Langtry Post Office

training was chosen to administer justice in the camp is a bit hard to fathom, but Bean got the nod. Once in office, he promptly burnt down the saloon of a Jewish competitor, and renamed the camp Vinegaroon, perhaps a testament to the rot-gut wine he served. He then called himself the "Law West of the Pecos River" and went to work as a magistrate administering justice from a 1879 edition of Revised Statues of Texas.

Judge Roy Bean's Courtroom and Saloon in Langtry

As the railroad got built, the camp moved along with its justice department and eventually wound up in Langtry, Texas where Bean built a proper saloon, selected jurors from saloon patrons, and refused to allow hung juries or appeals. Trials were often recessed, and during the recess all jurors were expected to buy a drink from his saloon. He only condemned two men to death, one of whom escaped before the sentence could be carried out. Horse thieves, usually sentenced to death in Texas, were all released by Bean if the horse was returned, which it usually was since the thief was often caught while riding it. Most guilty parties were fined, most fines were based on the amount of cash carried by the miscreant, and all monies collected went right into Bean's pocket - no surprise there.

The State of Texas chose to celebrate Bean's life with a museum where we Coasters were treated to a replica of Bean's saloon and courtroom. Court was often held on the porch in front of the saloon while drinks continued to be served in the barroom behind. In retrospect, it was clear Roy Bean had a romantic heart and a sound understanding of domestic conflict. He was the only judge in Texas at the time to grant divorces. He also had a good sense of appropriate application of the law, as his rulings were fast and fair. We could all benefit from more judges like Phantly Roy Bean, Jr.

 Along our route this day I saw road kill everywhere, including three fresh deer kills plus numerous corpses hidden along the roadside that I could smell as I approached. The deer kills didn't surprise me after seeing all the deer at the US Border Patrol Station, but what did surprise me was the prevalence of rattlesnakes. There seemed to be so many, yet there seemed to be so little upon which a rattlesnake could feed. I chanced upon a dead rattlesnake on the side of the road whose rattles had been cut off. One of our members, Dan, when taking a bio break on a bush, was startled by the head of a rattlesnake looming out of the bush at him its tail whirring mightily. Apparently it didn't relish the medium in which it was getting bathed.

Crossing the Pecos River was a bit hairy, as the bridge was narrow, long, and dangerous if you were a cyclist. The Pecos River used to be a roaring, raging waterway capable of creating the deep gorge through which it flowed. It is now less turbulent and feeds into the Rio Grande just north of the Armistad National Reservoir, a huge dammed up recreational area available to both Mexico and the US. The border of the two countries runs right through the middle of it, a deal made when the dam was built since a large portion of the resulting flooded area was destined be in Mexico. It certainly seems an easy way to enter the US, and I'd love to get

Jeff, Bob, and Joe Overlooking the Pecos

the official US Border Patrol spin on how they cope with intruders crossing into Texas from the reservoir. I doubt their efforts are very effective.

We camped at Seminole Canyon State Park under cloudy skies and strong winds from the east. Our tents were set up in and among scrub brush that seemed to be an inviting habitat for rattlesnakes. Consequently, I walked very carefully and gingerly on my way to the dinner table, making lots of noise with my feet. If I had to live permanently in Texas, my feet would be permanently shod with a pair of extra heavy duty Tony Lama cowboy boots as a protection against the dreaded fangs. I had dreaded those fangs ever since I lived as a youngster in Golden Colorado. My parents must also have dreaded those fangs, because they outfitted me with a snake bite kit in case I got nailed on one of my numerous hikes in the mountains. This kit had a nasty pointed knife for making a deep "X" incision at each fang point. Once the cut was made, there were a couple of suction cups for sucking out the venom. Times have changed though, and these kits are out of favor. Apparently there were far more fatalities from people cutting arteries and bleeding to death than ever died from the snake venom, so now the appropriate remedy is simply to keep the person calm (yeah, right!) and get medical help as soon as possible. As a kid I always wondered if I could have cut myself as so indicated.

Tent Site in the Seminole Park

I've mentioned our SAG team who provided organized stopping places along the route about every twenty to twenty-five miles, lifts in vans to those who couldn't go any further, and repository for excess clothing removed as the temperatures during the day rose. Each night, cyclists who had left something in the repository, were reminded to pick it up, but there was always something left over. Well this night, lo and behold, there was a sports bra in the SAG bin, and when Joyce held it up to be claimed, a voice in the audience cried out, "I wish I'd been there when they took that off" to the customary hoots and hollers. Then another voice offered, "That was a REAL sag stop," and the house came down. What a joy it was to be with such a humorous, congenial group. I think the sports bra just might have been a plant with the voices in the crowd scripted in advance, but the scene took everyone by surprise and was quite comical.

In addition to being humorous and congenial we all felt a sense of caring for each other. Everyone was reassured to know if they got into trouble with a bicycle problem, personal problem or accident, the whole group would pitch in to help out. It was most comforting.

Roadside pickup today was a **Child's Swim Fin**

March 30 - Day 24

Comstock to Bracketville
73 Miles

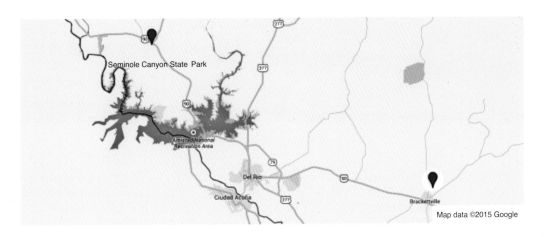

Map data ©2015 Google

A warm east wind blew through the Seminole State Park in the a.m., not the most propitious direction for cycling east, but the warmth of it took out some of the sting. It was overcast so the morning stayed warm without getting boiling hot. We were again exposed to chipseal pavement along with head winds, but I counted my blessings I wasn't also exposed to cold temperatures. The landscape consisted of gently rolling hills

Highway 90 Headed East

that kept rolling and rolling and rolling until they reached the Highway 90 bridge over the Armistad Reservoir. There a SAG stop was organized where we were joined by two Pecos County sheriff deputies. Bubba had let them know we Coasters were coming, and, since the bridge was too narrow for two passing semi trailers and a bicycle, they were there to escort us. We waited until about half our contingent had assembled, and then we set out with one escort vehicle ahead, blue lights flashing, and one escort vehicle behind, blue lights flashing. All traffic was stopped in the easterly direction as we consumed the entire lane. It was a hoot.

Sheriff's Escort on Highway 90

After crossing the Armistad Reservoir the next stop was the city of Del Rio, where we stopped for lunch. Del Rio in Spanish means "of the river" which seemed a bit of an odd name for a city, but the town was originally named San Felipe del Rio, which makes a lot more sense in Spanish. However, there was a San Felipe del Austin already in Texas, so when the government opened the first post office in San Felipe del Rio, they just cut off the San Felipe so that postal clerks wouldn't confuse the two towns.

Buying Air Mattresses at Walmart

Del Rio, with a population of 33,000, was the biggest city we had come to since El Paso, and my first stop was at the local Walmart to get resupplied with sun lotion, toothpaste, and flip flops. The Wolfpack was given instructions to clean out the entire stock of air mattresses since ours were deflating in the middle of the night at alarming rates. Air mattresses cannot be salvaged once they spring a leak, so the only recourse left to our pamperers was to replace them.

Next door to the Walmart was a fabulous West Texas barbecue joint called Randy's, where Tom, Linda, and I powered down the animal fat as rich, red barbecue sauce stained our riding jerseys. From Randy's we three pedaled, rattled, shook, and cursed the road surface for the next thirty miles, where there was little to see but the strange sight of a windmill with one blade that looked like it was made out of a mirror. I noticed it from a long way off, thinking the sun was hitting one of the metal blades at just the right angle. While all the rest of the blades were a dull rusty metal, this one shone brilliantly. It seemed to be catching the sun at just the right angle, but strangely enough, as I approached and my angle in relation to the blades changed, the brilliance of that one blade remained the same. It was eerie, and the eeriest part was none of the other riders saw it. I felt as if I had just ridden through the twilight zone. *Whoa,* maybe the hot sun and high desert air was getting to my brain. Maybe the ghost of a Spanish conquistador was sending me a message.

Ranch Entrance Framed in Yucca

There are many ranches in this part of Texas, and the owners tend to make the entrances to their estates noteworthy with sculptured metal frames showing off their cattle brands. One that I thought special was landscaped with Yucca cactus all in full bloom.

After Del Rio, the landscape slowly changed from dry desert to lush woodland. The bottlebrush acacia was in full bloom all across the land and was sending off a fragrance similar to honeysuckle. At times, it simply overwhelmed my senses with its luscious, sweet perfume. As I rode through these fragrant fogs it was easy to forget about chipseal pavement, pesky headwinds, and complaining crotches.

In the early afternoon, I arrived in Brackettville, home to a park that was once a major training area for cavalry called Fort Clark. It was established to train the troops commissioned to eradicate the Native American menace in the area. By the looks of things, Fort Clark was more of a day-camp than a serious venue for troop training with large officer homes, stone barracks, and an eighteen-hole golf course. It was now privately owned and run as a resort with a magnificent campground where we tented for the night.

Roadside pickup today was a **Heavy Bungie Cord Plus Three Smaller Ones**

March 31 - Day 25

Brackettville to Concan
72 Miles

Map data ©2015 Google

Linda and I headed out from Fort Clark at dawn, a grey dawn threatening rain. The temperature was in the sixties, but the east wind into which we were riding made it seem colder. We all bundled up against the elements knowing we would be able to strip down at the first SAG stop.

Eastward, Ever Eastward, in the Texas Hill Country

There weren't many photo ops on today's ride as the country, while greener than I had seen in weeks, and truly beautiful, was pretty much the same mile after mile. I did come upon a serious roadside memorial for a fallen rancher who got into a wreck with his pickup truck. I mentioned earlier that an interesting project might be to generate a photo album of these memorials. I then got to thinking (once all the photos had been taken and the deceased individuals identified, usually by inscriptions on the memorials), that graduate student research could begin on how each of them died. I did wonder when I saw the crosses and flowers how the victims met their doom. For instance, Roy Capps' memorial, whose picture I've included on the right, indicated he died in a pickup wreck, but what kind of wreck.?

Memorial to Roy Capps

Did he fall asleep at the wheel? Did an oncoming logging truck cross over the median strip and nail him head on? I think I mentioned that a cyclist has lots of time to let his mind wander while pedaling along, and my long suit is a wandering mind if you choose to believe my mother.

Uvalde was the only town of consequence along our route, and, fortunately, there was a Bank of America in Uvalde. I started this journey weeks before with three-hundred dollars in cash certain it would see me through the entire seven week tour, but here I was after week three with nothing left. If I'd thought for a minute before starting out about the expense of lunches, tips, and donations to worthy causes, I might have budgeted more realistically. I could have refilled my coffers from any ATM across the state, but there is something aggravating about all the fees charged which my bank, good old Bank of America, wouldn't charge me. Much to my astonishment, as soon as I put my card into the ATM slot requesting a large cash withdrawal, a bank employee emerged as if by magic next to me asking if my experience with the ATM was satisfactory. I had this sneaking suspicion they had a monitor in the bank, and whenever an out-of-state card was used, they sent someone out to verify its authenticity. I didn't mind at all knowing if my card was ever stolen the bank might be able to stop an illegal withdrawal. I later asked a bank executive if they ever did check on people using the ATM, and he said it certainly wasn't bank policy, and he didn't know if they could even identify a state when a debit card was inserted into the ATM. I got news for him, but I didn't press the point.

Ya Gotta Love Texas

As we left Uvalde we passed a classic west Texas marquee richly deserving of a picture. One hundred-thousand people are shot each year in America with about a third dying. I'm sure many of these shootings can be attributed to the combination promulgated by the message on this sign. We have a motorcycle shop in Keene advertising Bikes and Guns and it wouldn't surprise me if there was an auto dealership somewhere advertising Liquor and Cars. Connecting the dots between Liquor, Guns, and Vehicles gives rise to a level of suffering in this country that could so easily be avoided with a little common sense.

From Uvalde, we Coasters pedaled off into more hill country which, as one might suspect, is dotted with hills. Unfortunately, we hit more chipseal pavement that rattled my bike and drained my energy for the longest twenty-two miles I have ever ridden in my life. My strength left me, and I had to keep stopping for short breaks as much to allow fresh infusions of blood to my nether regions as to rest my legs. Along this route, I ran into several signs for Cowboy Churches, which again stimulated my wandering mind. What on Earth constituted a Cowboy Church? Can cowgirls go? Are all the pastors working cowboys? Cowboy was a term used exclusively for thieves, murderers, and

How About a Day Trader Church?

brigands back in the 1800s, so was a Cowboy Church dedicated to saving seriously wayward souls? Maybe the term Cowboy is a modern day euphemism for a serious crotch sufferer and there aren't any pews in a Cowboy Church so everyone prays standing. If a Cowboy Church had a cowboy for a pastor whose crotch howled and screamed as much as the crotches standing in the congregation, it might make his sermons more relevant to his suffering audience. Clearly my mother had a point about my wandering mind which seemed to wander a lot when I wondered!

Tom and Linda Relaxing

It seemed forever before I landed at Yeargan's River Bend RV Park, where the tour was camped for the night. The park wasn't limited to RVs as it had cabins, lodges, and tenting areas in addition to RV pads. There was also a well stocked general store carrying all the usual consumable items one consumes when on the road together with souvenirs of one's trip to west Texas. Just down from the lodge where I was staying was a fishing hole where Chester, one of the Wolfpack, managed to catch a fish of unknown origin. Further down toward the river, the tents were set up in one of the most idyllic camping settings I'd ever seen. In front of the cabin to which I was assigned was a patio swing where Tom, Linda, and I took turns rocking back and forth enjoying the pastoral views of white oaks dripping with Spanish moss and Chester lounging with his pole at the fishing hole. It was a warm, humid southern evening - a welcome departure from the dry, cold and windy desert nights experienced in the prior three weeks.

Idyllic Camp Setting at the River Bend

I didn't ever remember being so tired and thanked my lucky stars the next day was a rest day. Just lounging in the swing all day seemed like a pretty good idea at the time, but as it turned out, I made some interesting discoveries visiting the next town down the road, a town named Leakey. Right! How, I asked myself, did a town earn the name of Leakey?

Roadside pickup today was a **Man's Boot**

April 1 - Day 26

Concan
Rest Day

Yeargan's River Bend Park was located at the bend in the spring-fed Frio (cold in Spanish) River and the aforementioned campground was set up right at this bend. The park became a teeming vacationland in the summer as visitors came streaming in from all over Texas. I'll have to admit it's beautiful country, but I'm afraid its beauty would lose some if its appeal with hundreds of people listening to RAP on their boom boxes, drinking beer, and throwing their Big Gulp cups all over the place. Fortunately we arrived before vacation season and had the place pretty much to ourselves.

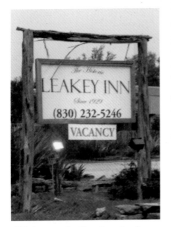

Welcome to the Leaky Inn

I slept late and lounged around all morning. Linda's daughter, Darcy, came to visit her from San Marcos, stayed for lunch, and then she, her daughter, Ruby, Linda and I went to visit Leakey, a neighboring town the locals all pronounce "Lakey." To the out-of-state uninformed visitor, a category in which I included myself, the town might bring to mind images of faucets dripping 24/7, roofs that didn't hold off the rain, and condoms that didn't prevent the next generation of Texans from being conceived. Our first experience with the cognitive dissonance brought on by this unfortunate name for a town was the Leakey Inn, not a place an uninformed visitor would automatically choose to stay if it were raining out.

Then we came upon Leakey Welding and, again, the dissonance to which my brain was subjected conjured up images of exploding gas lines and dripping oil storage tanks,. All these having been repaired at one time or another by a welder who didn't know how to weld, yet was proud enough to advertise his incompetence. These, of course, were grossly unfair conjurings but they made a good foil for hilarity in our group.

Look Out, It Might Leak

Having gotten as much milage out of Leakey as we could, sure enough we spotted a sign for "Real People Homes." This sign seemed to indicate there was a category of real people, as opposed to some other kind of people, to whom this agent was selling homes. If we the people aren't real, then what are we? Is Texas inhabited by aliens with whom this agent won't do business? We learned, of course, as we probed the environs for historical markers and questioned the locals, that Real meant royal in

Real People as Opposed to What?

Spanish, and a state senator named Julius Real represented Leakey at one time in the distant past. I read this on an historical marker outside the Real County Courthouse.

The four of us then wandered into The Friendly Grill to get an ice cream and met Ramona, who just happened to know Dick Walker, the "best fiddler in Texas." He, miracle of miracles, just happened to live in Leakey. I'm a bit ashamed to say I'd never heard of Dick Walker, and I learned much later that he had had an outstanding career as a musician with virtuoso capability on the violin, viola, mandolin, and piano.

Well, it wasn't long before Linda had talked Ramona into calling Dick and setting up a fiddling performance for the Coasters at River Bend that evening. By the time we arrived back at the park, Dick and contacted Bubba and the concert was all arranged. He arrived shortly before dinner, and we Coasters all enjoyed an evening of fiddle music, potbelly stove Texas yarns, and sing-alongs, all led by a truly remarkable man. This was a good lesson in demonstrating how amazing things come together if one just pays attention.

Dick Walker a Fiddlin'

An interesting side note for Country Western aficionados who are following the career of Camille Sanders is that Dick Walker was her first fiddle teacher when she was nine. He had just moved to Concan as a place to settle down for retirement when he met Camille and immediately recognized an outstanding talent. Dick told us what a quick study she was and what a delight she was to teach. Camille now sings and writes country western music and at the time had a recording on the Country Western Top Twenty. Her father, who manages the RV Park, gave us all one of Camille's CDs. Camille is now eighteen having performed professionally since she was fourteen. What a marvelous story!

It was an altogether lovely, restful day - all in preparation for another seventy-five miler up the steepest climb we would experience on the entire ride. *Ooooooh*, I just couldn't wait.

April 2 - Day 27

Concan to Kerrville
72 Miles
Halfway

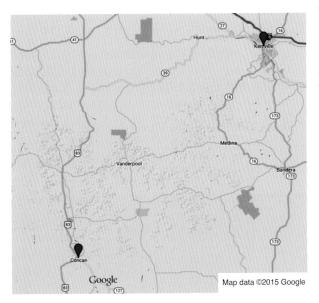

The weather had completely changed from hot (sometimes) dry desert to warm, humid uplands. It was overcast at dawn when we Coasters set out from Yeargan's River Bend RV Park heading back toward the town of Leakey visited with Linda's family the day before. The air was almost sticky as a warm mist swirled down the road - a mist that had a way of fogging up the the cycling glasses I wear to keep the sun, dust and bugs out of my eyes. When encountering fog like this while riding, I usually took my glasses off or rode with them perched on the end of my nose. Eventually the mist burned off so I could push my glasses back up where they belonged, but in the interim the only chance I took was with a bug flying into my exposed eyes. Cyclists had the same problem when riding in the rain, but fortunately sun, dust, and bugs intelligently stay home in inclement weather, unlike us intrepid cyclists.

I powered up one of the steepest hills of the entire tour on this day with my glasses down on my nose, my body bent, and head lowered as I slowly made my way up to the summit. Jeff then passed me like I was standing still and zoomed up to the top. I just don't know how these Tour-de-France types can go so fast up hill when I'm almost standing still forcing my legs up and down with all the energy I can muster.

Jurassic Park?

Once I reached the summit and admired the view all my hard work had provided for me, I headed out through the most picturesque country I had seen up to this point. Initially I rode through mile after mile of ranch lands, passing many ranches with very high fences designed to contain animals that normally would prefer not to be contained. Shooting exotic animals has been a sport enjoyed by hunters for generations, but as the exotic animals have been harder and harder to find in their natural habitats, Texas ranchers have risen to the challenge and provided preserves for them. Exotics such as wildebeests, zebra, ibex, and buffalo are examples of the many varieties of animal to be found on these preserves. There seem to be a plethora of fireplaces with empty space over their mantels just waiting to be garnished with a stuffed hippo head. I have a little trouble understanding the thrill of shooting fish in a barrel, but then, hey, I'm not a hunter.

I got a kick out of the entrance to one of these preserves which seemed to be offering up Tyrannosaurus Rex for the hunter's enjoyment. Calling this ranch a "Menagerie" seemed somehow fitting. Sad to say as earnestly as I peered through the fences, I didn't see anything more exotic than a scared jack rabbit and he was alongside the road. A terrified elk who had presumably escaped from a ranch, but then didn't have a clue what to do next, was seen by some cyclists running down the highway. As I write this there is a national furor over a dentist who has shot a pet lion in Africa. I'll bet now he wished he had gone to the Menagerie Ranch instead.

From the higher ranch land we descended to the Guadalupe River Valley and rode for miles along this meandering river, past beautiful homes and rambling estates. I passed one incredible house built out over the river that seemed like it must have been the handiwork of an inveterate stone mason. He appeared to be trying to make a spiritual statement out of stone, as there were several alcoves honoring Christ and Buddha. It just took one's breath away to appreciate such a rare and lovely structure in the middle of west Texas. Subsequent to crossing this river, Texas experienced some terrible floods, and the Guadalupe was one of the rivers impacted. I imagine the spot where I took this picture was flooded out, and I wonder as I sit here writing whether this lovely house is still standing.

Stone House on the Guadalupe

Just beyond the river crossing was the half-way point of the tour, 1,489 miles. Bubba's support team marked the exact point with arrows and, of course, we all stopped for photos. The picture is of Wayne Andresen, one of us who made an effort to write a daily blog and many of whose pictures I've used in this volume. Two days later, Wayne took a spill and broke his right arm forcing him to postpone completing the trip until the 2016 C2C. Falling off one's bike is always a hazard, and we were very lucky there weren't more accidents, considering the number of riders, miles ridden, and days on the road. Many of us had close calls. I almost went down in a construction zone when I hit a large piece of broken concrete that spun my front wheel out from under me, causing my bike to wobble mightily. I managed to stay upright, but had I gone down I'm sure I would have joined Wayne in the emergency room.

Wayne Andresen at the Halfway Point

The half-way site was framed on either side by a "boot fence". Every post on the fence had a worn boot capping it off. Nobody seemed to know how the placing of old boots on cedar fence posts got started, but post after post was now adorned with some sort of footwear. There were cowboy boots, engineer boots, lady's heels, sneakers, dress shoes, and sandals. Each shoe had a story and what an interesting story they could all tell. Were the shoes worn out, were they the wrong size, were they memorials to a deceased relative? Only those who placed them know, but it is fun to think of them as representing the souls of those who placed them on the posts. I only wish I had known about the fence so I could have brought along an old shoe to add to the collection.

Since I had gotten off to an early start from Concan, the day passed quickly and I was in Kerrville by early afternoon. I realized at one point in the journey, I had been averaging about ten miles per hour, not the thirteen I had originally thought. So at ten mph I could estimate a seventy-two mile ride would take about seven hours, and, indeed, this day it did.

Schreiner Park in Kerrville

Kerrville is a medium sized town with a population of 22,000 built along the banks of the Guadalupe River. It has been heralded as one of the wealthiest small towns in America with a diversified economy including a history of light manufacturing and wool distribution. A Frenchman, Howard Schreiner, started a business there buying wool from sheep ranchers, storing it, and selling it to weavers around the country. Using this business as a base, he branched off into cattle ranching, merchandizing, and banking. He was a philanthropist with his wealth and founded the Schreiner Institute, now Schreiner College, in Kerrville. The park, Schreiner Park, was established as a city park in 1930 and became a state park in 2004. It was a lovely, quiet setting along the Guadalupe River, a river that must have suffered recently from the flooding that hit west Texas.

I remember this park as the place I was able to share my Allopurinol with Udi. Allopurinol is an anti-gout medicine, and for those of you who have never been afflicted with the condition, you can bless your lucky stars you never have been and hope you never will be. There is no pain more excruciating as when "The Gout" descends, and it descended on my feet during one of my overseas assignments. I couldn't walk, I couldn't think, I couldn't do anything but writhe in pain until "The Gout" subsided. When Udi told me he had forgotten his meds to combat the condition, I immediately knew I beheld a kindred spirit, one with whom I could identify and render assistance. Fortunately I had plenty to spare. I'll never, ever, be anywhere without vast quantities of Allopurinol, just in case.

Roadside pickup today were **Two Deflated Metallic Balloons**

April 3 - Day 28

Kerrville to Blanco
59 Miles

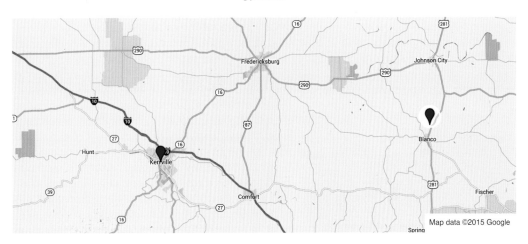

Map data ©2015 Google

Flood Gauge

The morning dawned warm and so humid it felt like rain at any minute. It was hard for me to understand how it could be so overcast, humid, and threatening rain, but not rain. I donned my rain gear expecting the worst, but the worst never happened, not to me anyway.

A different kind of worst did happen to me, though, right out of the gate. Unfortunately, my rear tire pressure had dropped to zero overnight, so I must have picked up a thorn or glass shard that caused a slow leak. I felt lucky I didn't have the flat en route the day before, as it's no fun changing a tire alongside a busy road. Fortunately, I had invested in a bag of super tubes and armadillo tires in El Paso, so Chandler changed my tire and tube before I set out. Sure enough we found a piece of glass that had worked its way through the old tire and into the tube. All gassed up (air is a gas) I set out across more of the Texas Hill Country

As I traveled through this hill country, I became aware of the danger flash floods filling the dry gulches with water during a heavy rain. These gulches often had flood gauges so that when they were full of water the uninformed motorist could make an appropriate decision about proceeding. It was a little hard to imagine a motorist risking being washed away in a rampaging torrent of flood water by entering such a dip in the road when it is clearly full, but it takes all kinds. At least with a gauge it would be evident how dee the water was so the motorist could assess the risk being taken.

The first SAG stop of the day was in Comfort, Texas, home of German Freethinkers who came there to settle in the mid 1800s. According to the Historical Marker, Freethinkers valued freedom of speech, freedom of assembly, and separation of church and state. They advocated equal rights for all persons, and their moral values were dominated by respect for life and nature. Comfort was founded by Ernst Altgelt in 1854 and was referred to as "Gemultlchkeit", a German word signifying acceptance, a notion of belonging, friendliness, coziness, and, comfort. Realizing it was an awkward word with which to name a town in English speaking America, it was simplified to Comfort. They rejected secession and advocated abolition of slavery, two positions making them at odds with the state's decision to side with the Confederacy. To avoid persecution for their abolitionist views, a large contingent of Freethinkers tried to migrate to Mexico to sit out the war, but they were chased down and slaughtered by the Confederate army at the Battle of the Nueces River.

Comfort Inn?

Comfort was a lovely place with stone buildings, bustling boutiques, and quaint delis. All across this part of Texas, I encountered the influence of Latinos, and Comfort was no exception. As I rode into our first SAG stop for the day at a Comfort deli, I announced my arrival in a booming, "Sambo el bueno esta aqui," (Sam the good is here), and I heard a laugh from a waitress standing in back of the patio. I found the diversity charming and wish we could explore ways to welcome our southern neighbors into our American community with less fear and loathing. As I left the SAG stop and headed out of town, a shop I passed advertised "Sophisticated Scintillating Specialties." If I'd had any interest in the kind of miscellaneous doo-dadery they exhibited on their front lawn, I would have stopped purely for the entertainment value.

From Comfort, I biked through the mist and humidity down seldom traveled backroads. It was a pleasant day and there was much to see, like when I passed a jet aircraft fuselage on someone's front lawn. Who would even consider wanting to own such an eyesore let alone go the expense of acquiring it and moving it to it's final resting place? Maybe it crash landed there.

The Aliens Are Coming, The Aliens Are Coming

Further along, I encountered a rusty farm implement. I think it was a planter of some sort, gracing a front lawn and clearly intended to be there for the enjoyment of passers-by. As Easter was fast approaching, it was adorned with colorful butterflies and plastic Easter eggs. I made a mental note thanking the occupants of the house for bringing such visual pleasure to my day.

The noon SAG stop was at the Sister Creek Winery, occupying a building once used to gin cotton. I mentioned

Lawn Pot Pourri

VIN E YARDS?

previously I didn't think of Texas as wine country, but Texas seems quite proud to be the fourth largest producer of wine in the states. The fact that it only represents about point two percent of total wine production in the country doesn't seem to deter their enthusiasm. We tend to think of whiskey as being what Texas cowboys would prefer to a glass of wine, and this perspective wasn't lost on the viniculturists seeking a market for their product. In the Friendly Grill we got a laugh out of an old-time advertisement: "WINE, What Classy Women Drink to get Wasted."

Further along our route we crossed the Blanco River, a significant body of water that apparently was tapped to supply the largest collection of greenhouses I'd ever seen. There was a sign indicating that the greenhouses were used to grow flowers destined for flower shops throughout the country. I pulled into the parking lot hoping to view a thriving operation only to discover the entire enterprise had been abandoned. Growing flowers for wholesale distribution must be a tough business, but I have this feeling as soon as Texas legalizes marijuana these greenhouses are going to spring to life.

Before our final stop for the night at Blanco State Park Campground, several of us paused at the local Dairy Queen for a root beer float fix. There is nothing, nothing, more satisfying than a root beer float after a day of biking. From the DQ we entered the park, crossed the dammed up Blanco River where children were merrily frolicking in the water, and fell onto our air mattresses. Facilities at the park were exemplary with plenty of hot water for showers, clean rest rooms, and ample covered space harboring picnic tables and barbecue pits. Since April when we Coasters stayed in the park, rains have inundated this part of Texas, the Blanco River has flooded out the park, and all the facilities have been washed away. I shudder to think what might have happened to us had the flood occurred during our stay at the park

Roadside pickup today were **Several Single Gloves**

April 4 - Day 29

Blanco to Lockhart
62 Miles

The temperature dropped twenty degrees overnight and never got much above sixty all day. It was overcast to start, with rain in the forecast, so I bundled up in warm riding gear and slickers. The rain never did come but it stayed cool and windy most of the day. The countryside between Blanco and Lockhart was a mix of woods, ranches, and agriculture. It was never boring, which made the ride quite pleasant.

Texas Equestrian Event - No Cowboys Here

We passed a horse show along our route where many of us Coasters stopped to chat with the participants. It was a "Hunter-Jumper" show with most participants being young ladies. I have always associated Texas horsemanship with calf roping, bronco busting, and barrel racing, so seeing an entire estate devoted to hunters, jumpers, and dressage came as a bit of a surprise. According to the bel canto farms sign we weren't welcome except by appointment, but nobody seemed to take much notice of us except one man who was curious about the C2C. He was a cyclist and wanted to know all about our journey. It's interesting to me that so few boys take an interest in classical horsemanship. Maybe if it was a bull-roping, hog-tying festival there would be better representation by the testosterone crowd.

Actually We Felt Quite Welcome

Texas Pie Company

Lunch was planned in Kyle at The Texas Pie Company, but pie isn't really my thing so I begged off and settled for a lunch of one protein bar and a swig of Gatorade. Riding on a full stomach seemed to sap my energy, so foregoing a double cheeseburger, large fries, and wedge of pie made a certain sense to me.

"Walking Beam" Oil Well Pump

A few miles outside of Kyle, I saw the first signs of the natural resource for which Texas is famous - oil. The clue was a "walking beam" pump that slowly and methodically lifted a gallon or so of oil out of the ground with each stroke. The line dropping from the head of the pump is called a sucker rod, and goes down to a simple piston pump in the bottom of the well. The beam then "walks" up and down pulling the sucker rod up, and sucking the oil out of the ground with each stroke. I had a friend once in California who told me stories of climbing on top walking beam pumps in Bakersfield and riding them up and down, usually after a night of drinking. I wonder if he's still alive. The oil from reservoirs requiring down hole pumps isn't under enough pressure to push the oil to the surface, so the pumps are required. Many oil reservoirs, however, are under so much pressure that the oil spews to the surface in huge gushers called "blow-outs."

On I ambled from Kyle to Lockhart where we Coasters were spending the night at the Lockhart State Park Campground. Lockhart is famous for its four barbecue restaurants and was named the Barbecue Capital of Texas by the state legislature. In the early days, Lockhart became a place where cattle herds from all over the west converged prior to taking the trail north to Chicago slaughter houses. Lockhart is the center of Caldwell County where the cornerstone of the Caldwell County Courthouse was laid on August 15, 1893. It featured mansard roofs, a high central tower, and a four way Seth Thomas clock. The original courthouse had no indoor plumbing, but, when the concept of

Caldwell County Courthouse

reached Texas, broom closets in the courthouse were converted into restrooms. It is said that when the first water bill was received, the county judge was so shocked at the charges, he padlocked the restrooms. I searched the Internet, but found no indication of what the occupants did to relieve themselves during those trying times. This courthouse in Lockhart is a spectacular example of 18th century architecture.

Some members of the group stopped at the famous barbecue restaurants for lunch while others of us went right to the Lockhart State Park where we were camping for the night. The park was huge with facilities for all kinds of overnight accommodations from tent spots to RV pads to cabins. It also had a golf course where a few of the Coasters hoped to play a round at the end of the day. I don't know if their wishes ever came true, and I suspect they didn't. Playing a round of golf after cycling for sixty miles sounds a bit much, to me anyway, as I flopped on my mattress as soon as I made it to camp.

Sad to say, this was the day Wayne, a photographer extraordinaire and delightful addition to our group, took a spill. We learned at dinner he broke his arm and wound up in the ER diagnosed with multiple fractures. His ride was over and we wouldn't see him again. Sadly enough we learned too that his daughter who had come out to visit him and ride a ways with us, had taken a spill on her first day out and cut her leg to the tune of eight stitches. Karma anybody?

Roadside pickup for the day were **Red and Yellow Road Reflectors**

April 5 - Day 31 Easter Sunday

Lockhart to La Grange
60 Miles

Map data ©2015 Google

It poured during the night for about an hour, so I looked forward to a day of clearing weather and warm, cloudless skies. No such luck. A gloom hung over the campsite on this happy Easter morning with breakfast served outside under a heavy, dripping mist. I was awakened by the mating call of an owl about five am, a call that sounded so much like a boy tooting a plastic horn I was certain it was a belated April Fool prank by one of our merrier cyclists. Ed held an Easter Sunday devotional and Cecil sang Amazing Grace as we all bowed our heads and thanked our lucky stars we had made it this far. Of course Wayne didn't make it this far, so it does make one wonder. We said a prayer for his speedy recovery.

Ed is a gentle man of great faith in the lord. It's a faith I don't share, not that I don't think there is something amazing going on, just that I don't understand all the human misery on Earth being tolerated by an almighty power who, if it truly is almighty, wouldn't put a stop to it. These Sunday devotionals he conducted had the effect of bringing all of us who attended together in spirit, a testament to Ed's faith that all things are possible. If Ed were pastor at a local church in Keene where I call home, I'd be the first to attend.

Now, this was Easter, the day Christ rose from his tomb, and a day I used to look for colored eggs hidden by an Easter Bunny. Did you know that the idea of an Easter Bunny came from Germany where it wasn't a bunny, but a hare? Hares were thought to be hermaphrodites who could reproduce without losing their virginity, so the Lutherans associated them with the Virgin Mary. This seems a bit of a jump, but at least the association between Christianity and rabbits is starting to make sense. Did you also know that this German hare was supposed to know which child was naughty and which was nice and only give eggs to the nice ones? And eggs, why eggs? Well it appears eggs were given up for Lent (forty-four days) by these immigrant Germans, and to keep them from spoiling they were boiled and then decorated as a festive punctuation to an otherwise penurious period. So the image of a happy hare hopping around with a basket of colorful eggs handing them out to delighted, nice children became part of American lore, and with the passing of time, the hare became a bunny, the eggs became chocolate, and all the children became nice.

As I left my tent that Easter morning, I found some plastic Easter eggs filled with candy together with fuzzy toy Easter bunnies sitting outside. Some of us, me included, tied the Easter bunnies to our riding helmets to emphasize the mood. Then, sure enough, someone brought a blow-

up plastic bunny that served as a photo-op centerpiece for the group. Notice how happy the two cyclists in the photo look as they anticipate their forthcoming sixty odd miles in the rain.

Happy Easter

Tom, Easter Bunny, and Your Author

After breakfast, eaten standing up as the mist circled around, I headed out of Lockhart Park destined for La Grange. The rain in Texas had brought out the wild flowers, and there were acres and acres of them blooming along our route. Picture taking was made difficult by the steady rain as I didn't want to get my iPhone soaked, but this one I couldn't resist.

One benefit to the dark, overcast days was the spectacular visibility of our bike lights, some of which can be seen for miles. Unfortunately, not everyone had good lights. The worst are those run on disposable batteries, since the cyclist never knows when a battery is getting low and needs to be changed out. The light will get weaker and weaker making it harder for passing motorists to see you. The lights

Texas Bluebonnets

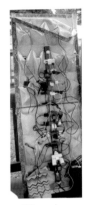
Charging

powered by rechargeable batteries are best, as they can be charged up every night along with iPhones, iPads, laptops, and electric toothbrushes. Bubba provided two large charging panels at every overnight stop with multiple sockets, where we could plug in our electronics. All of us were encouraged to turn off our units before plugging them in after the first night in a gym when the beeping and ringing of units left on kept many awake.

My miserable mood caused by the weather was lifted when I came across a witch who had flown into a telephone pole. It was such a delight to witness the playful nature some people express with their roadside creations. I would love to meet the person who did this one. I'll bet he or she was a mischievous child and a hoot as an adult. My kind of person to be sure.

This night we were camped inside at the La Grange recreation center gymnasium. It was such a relief to take a hot shower and put on warm, dry clothes. La Grange, if you keep up with Broadway musicals, was famous for its brothel; a brothel which, considering all the brothels that surely dotted the landscape in the wild frontier, must have really been something to have found its way into Texas lore. The musical was entitled "The Best Little Whorehouse in Texas," and was very popular back in the late seventies when it ran for 1,538 performances. The musical was made into a really bad movie with Dolly Parton playing the bosomy madam, Miss Mona, and Burt Reynolds playing the sheriff, Ed Earl, who looks the other way. I tried to watch it once when it was on TV, but didn't get very far before I began surfing channels looking for something, anything, better.

Wicked Witch No More

After dinner, Astronaut Captain Bill McArthur who has made three trips to the International space station, gave us a talk on his experiences in space. His talk was interesting, made more so with some great slides, but for some strange reason it struck me as all passé. I remember the time when every trip to space was such a special occasion and how we knew the names of all the astronauts. I was a bit embarrassed to say I'd never heard of Captain McArthur, but that was probably because I wasn't paying attention to American exploits in space after the moon shot. McArthur made an impassioned pitch for us to write our representatives asking for more money for space exploration, money that is continually being cut out of the federal budget. He is keen to use the increased budget to settle humans on Mars, basing his position on the rationale that humans would then survive in case an asteroid hits the Earth and wipes us out down here. It wasn't made clear what the survivors would do on Mars or how long they would be able to survive without Earth's backup. I could think of better ways to spend a trillion dollars, but I kept my mouth shut in deference to the captain who was a pretty neat, all-together guy. He was also a cyclist, a very strong one at that, and he rode with us on our way to Richards on Monday.

Roadside pickup this day was a **School Jacket**

April 6 - Day 31

La Grange to Richards
89 Miles

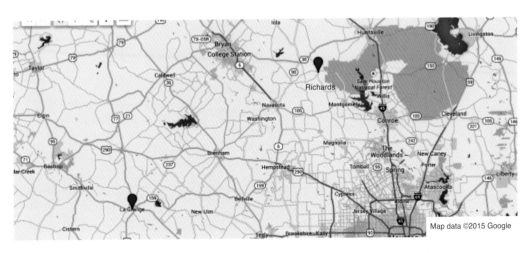
Map data ©2015 Google

This Monday of April 6th was warm, humid and threatening rain again, but we were assured if we got going early we'd beat the rain to Richards. So I headed out in the grey dawn with my red tail light strobing brilliantly to warn passing traffic of my presence and my colorful Easter bunny strapped to my helmet. Right off the bat, Dean had a cardiac event and stopped by the side of the road unable to catch his breath. Marla was marvelous in the way she took command of the situation, making sure Dean took it easy until the ambulance got to him. He was hustled off to the hospital where it was determined his event was not life threatening, but it would require some corrective measures. He was outfitted with a stent and rejoined the tour a week later in Shepherd, Texas. After another week he was back on his bike and riding as strong as ever. Dean was an inspiration to us all, but his experience did serve to remind us we aren't getting any younger.

Easter Protection

One of the first sights of interest I passed during the day was a cemetery just loaded with fresh flowers. I supposed they were all refreshed for the Easter celebrations, but it spoke volumes about the congregation and the respect they felt for their departed. I had seen many cemeteries, but few as well taken care of as the one here.

Texas Cemetery

Texas Longhorn

Ever since I read a James Michener book about Texas, I'd thought the long horn cattle had disappeared, but, lo and behold, there are actually quite a few ranches that raise them. I saw several fields with longhorns lowing in them, and as soon as I thought about cattle lowing, I realized I didn't have the faintest idea what lowing was. As a kid I thought it meant they were lying low to the ground, and never did question my childhood understanding. I Googled it that night to discover that cows "moo" while cattle "low" - same sound, different word. Go figure. I was told longhorns are raised as pets because their meat is tough and sinewy. Somehow a herd of two thousand pound pets leaves one willing to question the sanity of the rancher. Later, I was told longhorn meat isn't any different from other steer meat, but chances are I'll never have the pleasure of a taste test.

One thing I don't think I'd ever get used to is the sheer volume of road kill that exists along Texas roads. As I mentioned, most pickups have wrap-around tubular steel guards that protect the grille when a deer is broadsided. The deer carcasses don't seem to be picked up but are just pulled to the side of the road where the turkey buzzards pick off the sirloin tips. The rest is left to rot, and there was nothing like being on a bike to pick up the stench of rotting deer innards. I finally managed to get a picture of a couple of turkey buzzards working over a squished armadillo.

Buzzards Pecking Away

This was the day the tour went through Independence Texas, birthplace of the Lone Star State, which started off as a republic when Sam Houston's rag-tag band of desperadoes beat Santa Ana's Mexican Army at Independence. Santa Ana was captured and purchased his freedom by giving Texas to Sam and promising never to return. Santa Ana then returned to Mexico, but the nation was broke - a condition leading to his decision to sell off part of Mexico to James Gadsden in 1853.

What's Left of the Original Baylor College

SAG prepared lunch at a park outside Independence, where there were some typical buildings depicting the era. Independence was the first site of Baylor College, one of the early colleges established expressly for women. It's now in Waco, but the columns from the first building have been restored in Independence at its original location.

The last significant stop was in Navisota in front of the town hall, where stands a bronze statue of Frank Hamer, the epitome Texas Ranger who was honest, brave, incorruptible, etc., and best known for tracking down Bonnie and Clyde. He was conflicted in this assignment, since honest, brave, incorruptible Texas Rangers never shoot unarmed men and never, ever, shoot women. Apparently he did both when fulfilling his Bonnie and Clyde mission.

And there was always the scene of several cyclists pondering the problem of a flat tire. Cecil had one this day and Tom stopped to help him. We always thought we would have all the tools we needed to change a flat, but sometimes we came up short. Cecil had a bag of tools, but the one he really needed was a pair of tweezers to pull the tiny piece of steel wire out of his tire that caused the flat in the first place, and he didn't have it. He ended up covering the sharp end sticking inside the tire with a patch and limping into the SAG stop where our mechanic was waiting for him. Later, I bought a handful of tweezers at a CVS and handed them out to those in need.

Fearless Frank

It was a very long day, but the ride went through some beautiful country. To make it special, the rain held off and we had a tail wind most of the day. Even so, my legs slowly gave out as the miles passed under me and the last ten to the Mexican Hill Ranch, where we were tenting for the night, were a tough trek. I was so looking forward to the upcoming rest day at the ranch and reconnecting with an old friend from my days in the oil exploration business who was coming to visit me.

Roadside pickup today was **A Padlock**

Cecil and Tom

April 7 - Day 32

Richards
Rest Day

Rest days were languid interludes when we paid respect to our tired muscles and did as little as possible, and Bubba could not have picked a more delightful spot than the Mexican Hill Ranch outside Richardson Texas. The Ranch was a biker's haven overlooking rolling Texas rangeland populated with cattle, mules, and modest ranch houses. We were warmly welcomed by Earnest and Doris Bazan with a marquee designed just for us Coasters. One pink sign indicated San Diego was 1,839 miles to the west and St. Augustine was 1,220 miles to the east. The ranch also catered to nomadic motorcyclists, but this day it was all ours, and indeed, we felt warmly welcomed.

The Wolfpack set up our tents on sites around a central gathering spot, consisting of a recreation center that opened onto a patio shelter where we lounged to take our meals protected from from the hot Texas sun. The whole tour arrived just in time to catch the winner-take-all finals of the NCAA basketball tournament between Duke and Wisconsin off the wide screen TV in the recreation center. Duke managed to squeak out a win amid hoots, cheers, yells from those who cared enough to watch.

Marquee at Mexican Hill

An elevated swimming pool sat to one side of the patio where a sign was posted with strict regulations for those wishing to take a dip. The sign was clearly directed toward bikers of the motorized persuasion, as it was entitled, "Check Point Harley," and we took heart in realizing the rules were more than likely directed at this motorized, V-Twin nomadic contingent and not us. Never would a cyclist dream of making loud noises, engaging in dangerous horseplay, or peeing in the pool. However, some of us male riders stayed around after dark to see if any women in the group wanted to take a late night dip. Note that swimsuits are not allowed after dark if you're female.

Pool Rules

Overlooking the patio was a gazebo with a bench swing we took turns occupying. Here are six of the ladies, all of whom inspired us males with their courage and determination to cross America by bike. Sitting on the left is Loren who rode a recumbent bicycle and was making the trip with her husband ,Dave. On the swing are Marla and Gail who rode as a team and dazzled us all with their cycling strength and uncanny ability to find a

Loren, Marla, Gail, Barb, Lisa, and Monica

Starbucks in the most unlikely of places. Barb, next on the swing, was noted for being the most colorful rider on the tour, always adorning her helmet with some form of whimsical finery. Lisa is seated next. She was the one making the tour with her husband, Jeff, in support of Custom Canines. Standing is Monica, a geophysicist from Canada. She worked in the oil industry, as I once did, and we enjoyed talking about topics common to our professions.

Breakfast on rest days was huge with scrambled eggs, bacon, sausage, grits, yoghurt, bagels etc. etc. etc. Of course this was the day we did nothing so it was not like we needed vast quantities of calories, but I, and maybe others, thought we deserved to pig out because we had worked so hard. In general on these rest days, I proceeded to eat too much at breakfast, then eat too much at lunch and finally wolfed down Anne's huge gourmet dinner. If my body needed anything in the way of nourishment to get rejuvenated, it sure got it on rest days.

Hay Ride

Following breakfast, the Bazans organized a hay ride for anyone who might be interested. My interest was limited to taking a picture of those who were. I'd been around enough hay in my life, cutting it, bailing it, throwing it onto hay wagons and loading it into the barn to avoid it at every opportunity. However, everyone seemed to be having a good time climbing onto the wagon and joking about what used to happen during hay rides with high school sweethearts and contraband beer.

Chester

About every ten days, we would contract with a member of the Wolfpack to clean our bikes. It was Chester's turn this day. Chester was the indomitable spirit of the pack who was effervescent with a zest for life. He possessed a gift for holding audiences in rapt attention as he clowned around, and I told him he ought to try his hand at a career in acting. He reminded me a great deal of Eddy Murphy, and I believe he could easily have followed in Eddy's footsteps. At Augies RV Park I noticed the Wolfpack was pounding twelve-inch steel tent pegs with light claw hammers that made the job nearly impossible in the hard rocky ground. In gratitude for all they did for us, I purchased a couple of two pound sledge type beaters to do the job, and presented them to Chester as he cleaned Tom's bike. Chester beamed a huge smile from ear to ear and jumped into my arms, hugging me and expressing eternal thanks. He's was a hoot and a treasure to have on the tour.

All along the tour, friends of the cyclists would show up to visit us, congratulate us, and, no doubt want to check us out to see what kind of human would subject itself to such abuse. Bubba always made room for them at our meals and insisted we introduce them to the whole group. A couple who had stayed at Linda's bed and breakfast in Mexico, John and Karen Waddell, put in an appearance as did an old friend of mine, Vivian Dixon, whom I knew from my days drilling oil wells. Vivian and I spent three fun hours reminiscing and lamenting the loss of many wonderful friends we had back thirty years ago. I worked for Vivian's husband, Bill, and never had a more competent supervisor and mentor in my life. He passed away several years ago and I will always hold dear my memories of our interaction together running our company's oil service business in the far east.

After dinner John and Karen left, Vivian left, and I crawled into my tent and crashed, knowing I'd be back in the saddle at the crack of dawn.

April 8 - Day 33

Richards to Shepherd
62 Miles

Map data ©2015 Google

Almost the Santa Ana National Forest

It was a warm, humid day as we Coasters started out through the Sam Houston National Forest. It was a very special place, with towering pines and dense undergrowth making the ride most enjoyable. Logging trucks roared by, but generally they paid their respects by giving us the legal three feet. I had hoped to see a bear, or wildcat, or some interesting critter, but none appeared.

Tom Next to Genetically Engineered Steer

After leaving the forest, sights to see along the route were few and far between, but one of note we did encounter was a rather large steer announcing a ranch entrance. It's always fun to encounter Texas ranches and palatial homes sporting entrances enhanced with ornamental stone walls and ornate ironwork. This one certainly made a statement. In addition to the graduate student study of roadside memorials, another such study could focus on entrances to estates. We passed one after another as we tooled along.

This part of the South is known as the Bible Belt, and sure enough there are a plethora of small churches we ran into at about the same frequency as we ran into deer carcasses in the hill country, roadside memorials, and ranch entrances. I liked the marquee stationed at the Shepherd Family Worship Center that advised its congregation, "Don't Jump to Confusion." I see another graduate student project in the offing to document all the Bible Belt churches and their marquees.

Every now and again I came across a sight that stopped me in my tracks. The tree in the photo was one of those that was so unusual it was worth a snapshot. The bark was all gone, as if someone had peeled it off on purpose to create an art project.

The route to Shepherd wasn't particularly challenging, but there were some obstacles to circumnavigate and not all of us, namely me, didn't navigate them successfully. At one point, I had to make a decision to turn left or right at a "T" junction. I turned right and was merrily tooling along when a pickup truck pulled along side of me, and there was Dave, telling me I was going the wrong way. I happened to be riding alone at the time, and I never ventured to consult my route map,

Spooky Tree

trusting my acute intuitive skills to guide me, and sure enough I had turned the wrong way. Fortunately my taillight was strobing and my yellow shoes were flashing, so Dave and Ed spotted me as they arrived at the junction. After that I carried my route map in a plastic folder hanging in front of my handle bars, and I consulted it often.

Good Shepherd Sanctuary

This too was the day I rode through a construction site littered with chunks of broken up concrete. I had to thread my way through the chunks while cars, trucks, and construction vehicles passed me closely on the roadway. I mentioned earlier that, while checking my rearview mirror to see who might be approaching, I missed seeing a concrete chunk directly in my path. My front wheel hit it and snapped sideways throwing me off balance and almost causing me to go down. I shudder to think what might have happened if I had gone down, as all traffic was moving fast and dangerously close to the shoulder where I was riding. All's well that ends well.

The tour's stop for the night was at a most interesting place called the Shepherd Sanctuary. It was located just outside the town, and because it was run by two gentle, caring sisters, I wanted to believe the Shepherd referred to might be the Biblical Good Shepherd. These two ladies had created a place for wayfarers to stop and recoup their spiritual energies. There were camp sites, bunk rooms, showers, and a layout of fascinating artifacts created from curious objets d'art. One was a stick figure made out of discarded car parts. The head was from a flywheel adorned with spark plugs for hair. The arms were made out of piston connecting rods, the body from another flywheel, and the legs from scrap steel. I'm self aware enough to realize that the practical side of me could never envision such delightful, capricious, creative expressions having no empirical value. No wonder engineers have earned a reputation for harboring dull personalities.

Engine Objet d'Art

Another of these artifacts was an old Ford pickup bed and cab mounted onto a golf cart with a Massy-Ferguson tractor grille. Several Coasters took turns tooling around the grounds and taking pictures. Below is Tom hunkered over the wheel with his foot to the floor doing a blazing two miles per hour.

Geezer Tom Behind the Wheel

A wonderful cabin straight out of Grimm's Fairy Tales looked out over a fire pit where several of us gathered after dinner to chat until the bugs got to us. Another sight that startled me was an enormous pile of glass wine bottles. It looked like a garbage dump for

Grimm Abode

Ye Olde Bottle Pile

winos, but we learned the sisters were collecting enough bottles to construct a glass house. Perhaps it would be a part of the sanctuary available to those who normally throw stones and are seeking redemption in their lives.

Being a self styled do-it-yourselfer, I was just terribly impressed with the fact that these two gentle sisters had created all this by themselves. Clearly they were unimpeded by thoughts about doing things the "right way," but took off on their own to do them their way. Their way did sort of backfire on them, as after the C2C visited them last year, Bubba suggested they add more toilets which they did... their way. Unfortunately there are certain laws of hydraulics that need to be addressed when designing toilet systems, laws of which these gentle sisters appeared to be unaware, and problems occurred during the flushing of these new toilets. They were set up in a line, and when the contents of one toilet were flushed they tended to flow to a bowl of an adjoining toilet rather than the septic system. If you happened to be sitting on the adjoining toilet, the resulting eruption anointing your nether region was a most startling experience. The gentle sisters were horrified this was happening and promised to correct the condition for next year's arrivals ... hopefully by bringing in a licensed plumber.

One of the highlights of the day was the return of Dean, who had suffered the mild heart attack several days prior to. He elected to stay with the tour as his cardiologist gave him permission to rest for a week or so and then pick up where he left off riding with us. We all greeted him with hugs and warm, welcoming messages. He provided valued SAG support for a week, and then jumped back into the pedaling fray.

Roadside pickup for the day was a **Railroad Spike.**

April 9 - Day 34

Shepherd to Silsbee
61 Miles

Minimum?

It was curious to me that this ride through eastern Texas wasn't offering up the interesting sights along the road equal to those I saw further west. There were trees, green grass, trees, occasional road kill, more green grass and the ubiquitous single room Christian church. So I ground the miles off, pulling my head into my shoulders as the lumber trucks roared by. One heard how improbable it was to have two semi-trailers pass each other just where one happens to be riding, but it happens often enough to make for a thrilling ride. It was especially exciting when there was no paved shoulder and everyone driving a vehicle was making sure they obeyed the speed limit.

When the route was boring, I became more aware of my body and its reaction to the process of pedaling hour after hour. As I've mentioned previously, my awareness began with my body's contact with the seat. Little by little my nether region became sore, and the soreness wasn't relieved until I stood up and pedaled for a ways. As the nether region pain passesd I became aware of my legs losing their strength, and, as they did, they began to tell me it was time to stop. I'd try to ignore the pain, but I was reminded of screaming children, who, when you ignored them, only screamed louder. With gritted teeth I would pedal through the pain which would pass quite suddenly, surprisingly enough as my legs would regain their strength and my seat would feel mysteriously comfortable. Occasionally my back would join the chorus to take a break, but it too would give up its song as the waves of strength passed through my legs. These waves of strength and waves of pain I found all rather remarkable, and so different from the constant pain I felt at the beginning of the journey.

The one roadside sight that caught my attention this day was rows and rows of perfectly manicured bushes in a field outside Kountze. I asked the cook at the general store, who made me the best hamburger I had ever eaten, what was being grown and found it to be blueberries. My experience with blueberries ended as a child in Maine when we would take our white milk pails into the fields of wild blueberries and pick enough to put into our breakfast pancakes. I suppose I always knew blueberries were grown commercially somewhere, but just never associated the somewhere with Texas. This paralleled my ignorance of Texas viniculture as the fourth largest producer of wine in the US. Everybody should cross America by bike.

Blueberry Fields

Silsbee would be our last night in Texas and we had heard the last night in tents for a while. Silsbee was established in 1895 as a railroad stop in support of the Kirby Lumber Company and was named after Nathaniel Silsbee, who put up the money for the railroad. Bubba had reserved space for his Coasters at the Thompson RV park, a park that seemed to be just getting organized for the summer season with some amenities, namely the bathrooms, still being in a state of reconstruction. We were tenting, but Bubba had reserved four cabins with showers we cyclists could use. Well, it seems they had the dates wrong, the cabins were already rented to others, so all we had was one shower for thirty-two men and one separate shower for eleven women. All of us, of course, wanted to shower at about the same time.

The scene inside the men's rest room reminded me of the lineups at a deli counter without the numbered tags. We all knew who we were supposed to follow into the shower, so we slowly got undressed as our turn approached. Picture, if you will, a line of men standing in front of a shower curtain. The one in front of the line is naked and ready to jump into the shower as soon as the previous occupant pushes the curtain back. Each showerphile in the line is in a various stage of undress discarding clothes as the line inches forward. The mood is merry with taunts from the line like, "What are you doing in there?" and "How long does it take to soap up?" or "Don't hog all the hot." As one scrubbed, naked body left the shower stall another sweaty, naked body entered. At one point, the lights went out, and an extension cord was brought in to keep the place illuminated. In retrospect, it was all quite comical, but at the time a bit exasperating.

The park had a large pavilion overlooking a lake where Cecil celebrated his birthday by providing free margaritas to those who imbibed. Celebrants went through quite a few

Pavilion in the Thompson RV Park

bottles of Tequila with merriment increasing with each throwaway. We had three birthdays on the trip including Cecil's.

I might have mentioned that I don't like tenting. I suppose it was novel when I was a lad, but when faced with having to pee in the middle of the night, air mattresses going flat, and the total lack of space for organizing your kit, tenting sure loses it's appeal fast. For those of you who haven't ever tented before, try getting dressed while sitting on the floor of your bedroom while pawing through a large bag of jumbled up clothes. It's not only hard to find what you want to wear, but often harder to put it on, especially if it's a pair of pants. Bubba indicated we'd be tenting about half the time, and if we didn't like tenting then this might not be the right trek for us. He related one incident when a candidate told him he hated camping but would probably learn to like it by the end of the trip. Bubba's response was that if he hated camping before the trip started, he would hate it worse at the end of the trip and probably shouldn't come along. The candidate never did sign up. Now that the trip is over, I don't dislike tenting any more than I did before the trip started, but that's probably because I couldn't have disliked it any more than I did before the trip started.

But if Bubba ever asked me how things were going, my knee-jerk no-whine response was always, "Perfect in every way."

Roadside pickup for the day was a **Rusted Out Hammer from an Old Flintlock Rifle**

April 10 - Day 35

Sillsbee TX to DeRidder LA
73 Miles

Map data ©2015 Google

TX - LA Border

April 10th was the day we crossed the Sabine River, the boundary between Texas and Louisiana. Somewhere in the dark corners of my memory there is a something about Sabine women, abducted (raped?), by Romans looking for wives. Thus, Sabine seems like an odd name for anyone to choose for a river, unless, of course, there is a history of similar activities taking place along its shores. I Googled the origin of the name, was told by Wikipedia that sabine means "cypress" in Spanish, but no Spanish dictionary I consulted would own up to the translation. So much for my dependable straight skinny source.

There used to be a huge, multicolored sign welcoming everyone traveling Route 190 east into Louisiana, but all that remained of the sign were two four-by-four wooden posts. Apparently, the sign had been stolen as a couple of Coasters stopped at a tourist office to ask what happened to it, but the tourist office staff knew nothing about the missing sign and promised to let the authorities know. I held off until I rode across boundary between Louisiana and Mississippi, and then talked Tom into photographing me looking east. At least I got my state line welcome picture even if I was facing the wrong way.

Sam Looking East

The route to De Ridder along Route 190 was a blessing, as it had a wide shoulder we cyclists could use as one lumber truck after another roared past, showering the road with splinters and chunks of bark. There were a few cowboys who drove their lumber trucks right along the edge of the white line and then leaned on their air horn as they passed. These horns were frighteningly loud, and when, the sound of the horn was combined with the sound of eight diesel cylinders cranking at maximum RPM, the effect was terrifying. I was terrified but, on the bright side, my terror probably gave rise to the most enjoyment the driver had all day. I consoled myself by thinking I had done a good turn for some soul more miserable than I. Jeff had the temerity to talk to one of the drivers at a stop light and was told in no uncertain terms peppered with expletives that the trucks owned the road and we had no business being on them. I chatted with one of the drivers at a service station and found out they were all headed for pulp mills. He didn't seem to be particularly bothered by cyclists, unlike the one Jeff encountered. It takes all kinds.

Thistles

Daises?

The route was pastoral, so I amused myself by taking pictures of flowers. I thought the pink flowers on the thistles were particularly attractive, as were the beds of yellow daisy lookalikes.

Fausto's Terrific Fried Chicken

Some of us stopped in Merryville for lunch where, we had been told by Jeff and Lisa, Fausto's served up the best fried chicken they had ever eaten. Fausto's was a small restaurant that had been in its present location for twenty-two years, and the same crew that served Jeff and Lisa in 2014 served us again today. It seemed everything you purchased was fried, so we downed fried chicken, french fries, coleslaw and fried apple pie. Actually, the slaw wasn't fried, but who knows, maybe fried cabbage soaked in mayo would be pretty good. By the way, "kool", pronounced "cole" is Dutch for cabbage - did you know that?

Flat tires were sometimes a little hard to detect, especially if the road surface was this chipseal used so often in Texas. Your fillings rattled around so much in your head you might fail to realize your tube was rattling down the road too until it slithered sideways. It happened to me again today, and I must have driven a hundred yards before it dawned on me something was amiss. I was getting used to the idea of being pampered, so instead of changing my own tire, I immediately called Chandler, our mechanic, who showed up in about fifteen minutes and made quick work of getting me back on the road. This had now been my third flat. Neither Tom nor Linda had had one yet, but we'd been told by experienced coasters it was inevitable everyone would have at least one flat during the trip. They weren't wrong - we all did have at least one eventually. Cecil had fourteen!

Chandler Fixing Sam's Flat

Later on in the evening, Chandler had a rollover accident with his truck, the one you see in the photo, and totaled it. He was very fortunate to have survived the incident and, even though he declared himself to be "fine" at the scene, the first responders were required to pursue medical attention. They took Chandler to the ER, and the docs determined he had broken his back. He spent the night in the hospital but then rejoined the tour in a day or so, with a back brace and doctor's orders to minimize heavy lifting. Chandler let it be known that without a seat belt and air bags he would have surely been killed. It was looking like we'd be losing our mechanical support, but Murph stepped up to help Chandler with any heavy lifting.

Beauregard Parish Courthouse

This was another day we Coasters outraced the rain, and we pulled into De Ridder before the promised showers. De Ridder was named after Ella de Ridder, the sister-in-law of a Dutch railroad financier. The first house in the area was built in 1893 by Calvin Shirley, who homesteaded 160 acres. Then the railroad came through, the first saw mill was built, and De Ridder was eventually voted the Parish Seat of Beauregard Parish. Once it became the parish seat, De Ridder merited a courthouse - another building worthy of documentation and another testament to the high regard with which the deep south held law and order. Necessity, it seems, was the mother of invention here as it was most everywhere else.

We stayed in a Comfort Inn this first night in Louisiana. Bubba gave Anne, our chef, the night off, as he had found a marvelous restaurant where he was going to treat us all to our dinner. However when he checked on the reservation, the proprietor had the wrong week written down, so Bubba gave a local pizza parlor the biggest single order they'd probably ever received. Boxes and boxes of pizza arrived in the hotel parking lot where I pigged out on pepperoni, my favorite. I had ninety miles to ride in the coming day, so I felt perfectly justified in stuffing myself with Italy's most significant contribution to American culinary arts.

Roadside pickup today was a **Blue Bath Towel**

April 11 - Day 36

De Ridder to Opelousas
91 Miles

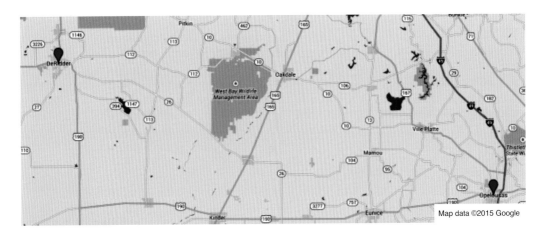

Map data ©2015 Google

Rumble, Rumble

The ride this day was enlivened somewhat by the rumble strips cut into the pavement along the shoulder. These are designed to wake up a sleeping motorist, but they played havoc with a wide awake cyclist. We hadn't encountered many roads with rumble strips so far on the trip, but they needed to be avoided, either by riding on the highway inside the white line, becoming a target for logging truck drivers, or riding outside the strips on what's left of the shoulder. Both approaches force a cyclist to pay greater attention as hitting one of the indentations unawares could cause a spill.

While paying close attention to the "rumble" in rumble strips, I still looked for sights that might bring an amusing thought to mind. With a church every mile or so through this "Bible Belt," I was most impressed with the fellow named Moses who was running for office. I wondered if he had changed his name when he decided to run. I mean, how could a passionate Bible lover not vote for Moses? I then began to think about other Biblical names when I almost ran over a dead Armadillo. They say nobody ever

How Could He Lose in the Bible Belt?

sees a live Armadillo, only dead ones on the road, but later on outside St. Francisville, a few of us saw a live one rummaging through the undergrowth. It was the only live one I had ever seen.

While we're on the subject of death, I knew they "buried" corpses above ground in New Orleans to keep the coffins from floating away during times of rising water tables, but I didn't know they did it everywhere in Louisiana. Today along this route, the cemeteries we passed seemed to hold their inventories in massive granite boxes protruding partially above ground. Maybe the granite was heavy enough to keep the contents from emerging. The idea of being able to lift a lid from time to time to see how your departed mother was doing sort of gives me the heebie-jeebies, but I doubt many people ever do that. We were, however, well below sea level during this ride as indicated by Tom's Garmin, so the heavy chambers were a necessity, as the water table either was, or was about to be, pretty close to the surface. It allowed me to contemplate accounts that all of Louisiana and most of Mississippi at one time were both part of an inland sea that slowly got silted in by the "Big Muddy."

Granite Coffins

Crawfish Harvesting

Soon thereafter, we came upon flooded rice field after flooded rice field, fields that also served as crawfish spawning grounds. The rice is planted, the fields are flooded, and then crawfish are seeded into the flooded fields much as trout streams are stocked. The rice and crawfish seem to flourish together, with both

providing a cash crop for the farmer. The crawfish burrow into the muck when the rice is harvested, and are then caught in baited traps.

The photo shows a scow powered by a stern wheel so it can slog its way through the shallow flooded fields to pick up the crawfish traps. You can see the buoy indicating the location of a trap that the farmer then picks up as he

Fly Spray

The rice fields are sprayed by plane, and I saw several at work coating the earth with insecticide. I followed one plane, waving madly as it flew past, and, in answer to my thirst for attention, the pilot made a low pass right next to me. In doing so he swooped over a tree, barely missed a telephone pole, broadcast his load over a corner rice paddy, and then darted almost straight up to miss a house. Whatever he was broadcasting on the rice got broadcast all over me as well, making me as insect free as the rice field he was treating. I suddenly got curious as to what would happen to a mosquito who stopped by my arm for lunch and sucked up a stinger full of methyl parathion or synthetic pyrethroid, two insecticides used in rice farming.

One of our memorable stops was for lunch in Mamou, a town famous for its Zydeco music. According to Wikipedia, Zydeco is a musical genre evolved in southwest Louisiana by French Creole speakers, which blends blues, rhythm and blues, and music indigenous to the Louisiana Creoles and the Native people of Louisiana. Supposedly the term "zydeco" derives from the French phrase, "Les haricots ne sont pas salés," which, when spoken in the Louisiana Creole French, sounds as "leh-zy-dee-co nuh sohn pah

Lisa Watching Marla Trip the Light Fantastic

salay." This literally translates as "the snap beans aren't salty," idiomatically as "I have no spicy news for you," and colloquially as "I'm so poor, I can't afford any salt meat for the beans." It was left to the imagination how snap beans got mixed up with music. Anyway, Fred's Lounge had carried on an old tradition of opening it's bar at eight Saturday morning and offering live Cajun music until one in the afternoon. I guess they figured everyone would be drunk by noon on Saturday anyway, so why not give them a place to congregate. The music was loud and, well, unique, and, yes, everyone seemed to be rather vacantly enjoying themselves. It was fun to watch the locals, mouths agape, not quite able to believe what they were seeing in attractive, slender ladies all decked out in cycling spandex kicking up their heels on the dance floor.

Our Coaster group had been lucky, as we met another bike group in Mamou who had been pummeled by rain the day before. We had dodged it so far.

From Mamou we biked on to Opelousas, one of the oldest cities in Louisiana and named for the Appaloosa Native American tribe that inhabited the area. It was a center of cotton production during its early history with huge estates and palatial homes. It fell into decline after the Civil War with the drop in cotton prices and elimination of slave labor, but rebounded somewhat during the era of Governor Huey Long as a destination for gamblers and prostitutes. Opelousas is now relatively prosperous with the coming of a Walmart distribution center, Evangeline Downs Racetrack, and numerous companies in light manufacturing. I headed directly for the Holiday Inn Express and hit my wonderful comfy bed for a much anticipated nap.

Roadside pickup for the day were **Two T-shirts and a Lady's Blouse**

April 12 - Day 37

Opelousas to St. Francisville
67 Miles

Map data ©2015 Google

It was pouring when we awoke so I steeled myself for a day's ride with water running down my neck, my wheels spinning rooster tails of silt up my back, and my feet inundated by waves from passing cars. By the time breakfast was over, however, the rain had slacked off, and it hardly rained any for the rest of the day. I kept thanking my lucky stars how unusually fortunate we'd been riding between fronts and missing all the messy weather.

I have this mental image of our northern states a million years ago, covered in glacial ice a mile thick, and the southern coastline terminating at about the boundary of Tennessee. I then roll this image forward with the ice melting, rivers forming, and sediments slowly creating the land masses we call Louisiana and Mississippi. Because these land masses were created by slow sedimentation rather than violent volcanic eruption or tectonic plates crashing into each other, the land is incredibly flat. Water running across flat land pretty much runs everywhere, and so it is in Louisiana with rivulets, streams, bayous, and rivers all meandering steadily southward to the Gulf of Mexico. We crossed one of these rivers, the Sabine, when we entered Louisiana and we were poised to cross another, the Atchafalaya, outside Opelousas at Krotz Springs.

Entering Atchafalaya

The sheer volume of water entering the South has given rise to vast swamps, one of which, the Atchafalaya National Heritage Area, we had to pass through before crossing the river itself. Route 190 crosses this swamp land on a long narrow causeway deemed so dangerous to cyclists that last year's C2C crossed it with a police escort. This year, however, we bypassed the bridge by taking the old road through the swamp. The old road was just that: a disused two-lane concrete way littered with the detritus of disuse and replete with broken pavement, dangerous tire grabbing cracks, and water-filled pot holes. Woody, one of the most experienced riders in the group, had a spill after hitting a crack, and wound up having to leave the tour. The spill aggravated an eye problem, which doctors deemed too serious to allow his continued riding. The road, however, was a hoot, as I had to ride slowly and carefully giving me time to watch for alligators and snakes. Lisa and Jeff saw an alligator. Lucky them.

Albert Waiting for Pogo

After crossing the litter strewn swamp bypass, the tour returned to Highway 190 for a couple of miles ,where we had our first SAG stop at a convenience store. It wasn't very convenient for a frantic Linda who, with her face drawn in panic, informed me she had lost her wallet. The velcro on her bicycle pouch had opened up as she bounced through the broken concrete, and her wallet had fallen out somewhere along the swamp road. She immediately summoned Margie's SAG vehicle to return down the swamp highway, in hopes that she could spot her wallet if they drove slowly enough. I agreed to ride back down Route 190 to see if it had fallen out along the highway. Just as I was turning out of the parking lot Marla was turning in and, as she did so, she held up the wallet and threw it in my direction. We both savored the moment when Linda would return, angst ridden and distraught, over not finding her wallet along the swamp road, and we would present it to her. She, of course was delighted, and pledged to find a new, more secure, place to carry her valuables. Clever lady.

The Atchafalaya River is a very big river and parallels the Mississippi River. Its headwaters appear to include the Red River as well as spurs to the Mississippi River, but once it departs from the Three Rivers Wildlife Management Area in northern Mississippi it runs to the Gulf of Mexico independent of the big muddy. Route 190 separated into to two lanes in each direction before the river, and two bridges over the Atchafalaya River at Krotz Springs carried two lanes each. As I cycled over the eastbound span, it was hard to believe this river wasn't the Mississippi. It is a huge river and it was rumored that Governor Huey Long chose the height of the original bridge, built in 1937, such that no ocean going vessels could pass under it. He wanted to make sure all commercial traffic was unable to follow the river into Mississippi and stayed in Louisiana, thereby boosting the river's economic potential to the state.

Once over the Atchafalaya, we soon came to the Mississippi, which we crossed over a relatively new suspension bridge. I had visions of the river being wider, but then I was looking at it from five hundred feet up, and if I had been standing on one shore looking across, it might have seemed bigger. It didn't seem much wider than the Atchafalaya and in fact wasn't at the point we crossed, both being about two miles across. I looked for the Robert E. Lee paddlewheeling its way through the shoals, but saw only a single barge. Both the Atchafalaya and the Mississippi were at flood stage from all the storms hammering the midwest that hadn't yet hammered us. The bridge shown in the photo is named after the famous ornithologist John James Audubon, who spent many years in

John James Audubon Bridge

New Orleans. The bridge is the second longest cable span in the Western Hemisphere, and no, the longest isn't the San Francisco Bay Bridge but the Baluarte Bridge, spanning the gorge separating Durango and Sinaloa, Mexico.

Dropping down on the other side of the Mississippi River brought us Coasters to the Louisiana town of St. Francisville, pop. roughly 2000, once a thriving cotton port during the pre Civil War era. Many cotton plantations lined the river in the early 1800's, and those that had been restored are tourist destinations for pre Civil War buffs.

Our stop for the night was at the Marydale Girl Scout Camp, a rambling acreage dotted with large cabins and multiple-berth bunk rooms located a few miles outside of town. This was the first time Bubba had arranged for

the C2C to stay at the camp, and because he hadn't had the opportunity to actually visit the Marydale site prior to our arrival there was a problem. While there was a beautiful recreation hall and kitchen at the entrance to the camp, some of the cabins were over a mile away from there. The road to these cabins, being gravel on a soggy dirt base, was impossible to navigate with a thin tire bicycles, so the occupants had to walk for half an hour each way. This didn't sit too well with many of the Coasters who, though sworn to continuous no-whine, happy faces, expressed their discontent in subtle ways discernible to Bubba's keen sensitivities. Soon, the Wolfpack was at work setting up tents around the beautiful recreation hall and kitchen, much to the delight of those whose cabins were a mile away. Unfortunately, the rains came the first night we were there and many of those who chose acceptable

Heading to the Cabins

proximity over cabin shelter got soaked, as the lawns where the tents were set up flooded out. There is an adage rattling around in my head about how tough it is to make all the people happy all the time. I think P. T. Barnum had something to do with it.

In writing my blog for the trip, I described the sleeping arrangements in the cabins as being in "multiple-birth" bunk beds. Obviously my brain was lacking the necessary oxygen after a long ride to think clearly, and my loyal fans reading this typo didn't hesitate to point out the irony of a girl scout camp providing the necessary facilities for multiple births.

Roadside pickup for the day were **Strands and Strands of Mardi Gras Beads**

April 13 - Day 38

St. Francisville, Louisiana
Rest Day

Marydale Camp was pure deep South with spectacular low-branched live oak trees laden with Spanish moss. The air was warm and saturated with moisture, which envelops one like a soft, fuzzy blanket. I loved it, but others weren't so comfortable. What a change from the ultra-dry air of the Sonoran desert.

Questions flowed about the nature of Spanish moss. Was it a parasite, draining trees of their sap, or was it in some sort of symbiotic relationship where the live oak needs it for survival? After a bit of "Googling," we discovered Spanish moss was an epiphyte - a plant getting all its nourishment from the air. Theoretically, it doesn't harm the tree, but it does prevent sun from getting to the leaves, thereby stunting the trees growth. Apparently, trees laden with the stuff blow down more easily in a hurricane, but who really knows?

Spanish Moss

It rained like crazy on the morning of April 13th, but by noon it cleared ,so Tom, Linda, Dan and I rode our bikes into St. Francisville. Before we set out, however, we all gathered around to look with amazement at Hans' rear tire. The tread layer had completely separated from the cord layer for a third of the circumference. Hans told us he had no sensation coming from his bike that anything was amiss until he got to the campground. The inner tube was still intact and fully inflated. Here we were ,all experiencing flat tires from teeny weeny metal wires penetrating our treads, and Hans managed to ride for miles on a tire literally falling apart. Wow!

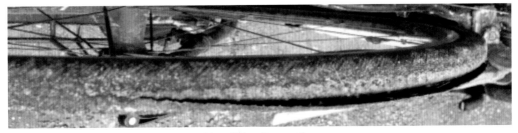

Hans' Tire Separation

Once a Huge Port

No one could have guessed, by only a quick visit, that St. Francisville, with a population of only around 2000 souls, was once a major port along the Mississippi. The Major port started as Bayou Sara, a protected inlet, that was at one time the largest port on the Mississippi between New Orleans and Memphis. Floods and fires kept destroying the town so the whole community was transported to a bluff downriver in 1920, where St. Francisville had stood since 1809. St. Francisville was the commercial and cultural center of the area ,whereas Bayou Sara was the port, a town with flourishing port facilities that completely disappeared with the drop in cotton prices following the Civil War. St. Francisville is now a tourist destination with a small museum, where three delightful southern ladies filled the four of us in on historic details. Dan and I then rode down the bluff and stood on the spot where so many years ago barges, laden with thousands of bales of cotton, were moored awaiting their turn to enter the Big Muddy. Nothing was left of the once bustling port of Bayou Sara.

The Docile Big Muddy - Looks Pretty Big from Here

West Feliciana Parish Courthouse

Dan and I then headed back up the bluff where we rode by some beautiful antebellum homes and a lovely old courthouse. St Francisville was made the seat of West Feliciana Parish in 1824, with this courthouse built shortly thereafter. The antebellum homes we rode by were imposing, but many screamed, "restore me" as their paint peeled and window sashes rotted. Restoration of historic buildings is a frighteningly expensive proposition, and few individuals have the resources on their own to do it. One home we passed by was being restored as a movie set and, of course, many antebellum homes are open to tourism and charge an admission that one might hope is sufficient to cover the cost of upkeep. Somehow it would be a shame if they all disappeared, because they do tell quite a tale about the early history of America. On the other hand they stand as a symbol of economic gains resulting from of America's support of slavery - support that will be forever a blight on the story of our nation.

Hands Off

On the way back from town I did a double take when I saw a sign indicating this was a "Hands-Free Zone" with profiles of two children. I'm embarrassed to say the first thought that popped into my head was an admonition to adults to keep their hands off children. This seemed a bit odd to put on a sign at a school zone, more the sort of thing one might find in a newspaper editorial, so what on Earth did it mean? Well, apparently there was a move afoot in the Louisiana legislature to prohibit the use of hand-held cell phones while driving, but conservatives didn't like the blanket nature of the bill, so they watered it down to only cover the use of cell phones in school zones. The watering continued to allow the use of cell phones in school zones provided they were "hand's-free." In this form the bill was passed. However, when tickets were first issued once the bill became law, someone was able to beat their rap by arguing the government needed to post signs in all school zones if they intended to cite motorists for breaking the law. So now all school zones in Louisiana have signs that say, "Hands-Free Zone." Isn't America great!

For dinner this night we had a real, live Cajun spread of crawfish, corn on the cob, and boiled potatoes. The crawfish were prepared by two chefs from St. Francisville, who arrived with their trailer-mounted cooker and barrels of fresh crawfish. Many of what we ate probably came from the rice fields we had gone through a couple of days before. Crawfish look just like midget lobsters, but the only part you eat is the tail that you suck out. For as many as most of us ate, there were piles of boiled crawfish left over, that the staff peeled and Anne made into a jambalaya for later consumption.

Crawfish to Go

Crawfish Soon to be Gone

The trip the following day was taking us eighty-two miles to Franklinton, so most of us turned in early. Heck, most of us turned in early anyway. Recall that the average age of us Coasters was sixty-three, so you need to cut us old folks some slack.

April 14 - Day 39

St. Francisville to Franklinton
86 Miles

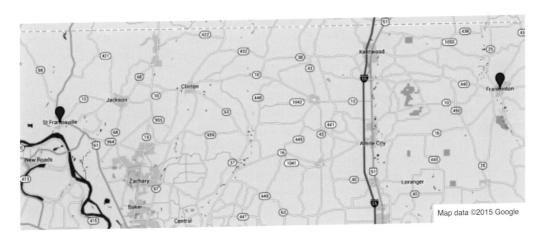

Map data ©2015 Google

Hot, Sweaty, Wet

We awoke this day to rolling thunder and the pitter patter of gentle droplets on our cabin roofs. The NOAA radar map showed a band of showers moving away from Maryville Camp, so I took heart that maybe the tour had dodged another rainy day. Well, no such luck. By the time Linda and I had hit the road it was raining steadily, so I bundled up in my yellow rain jacket and made ready to face the day. The rain jackets kept the rain off, but they also kept body heat in. Often wearing them in a warm, humid rain can create more misery than just getting wet. Some Coasters chose cool, natural wet to hot, sweaty wet and cycled without them.

It rained steadily for the first twenty miles with rolling thunder, giving the two of us hope that the storm was moving away when brilliant flashes and sharp claps gave pause to our hopes. The storm was clearly building and spreading its reach all along our route east. At one point, a lightning bolt and clap of thunder occurred so close together that Linda and I took a break under the eaves of a local church. Others with less fear of getting hit by lightening waved at us as they splashed by. What a day! At times, it rained so hard that the drops stung our cheeks and rivulets of runoff traveled down the edge of the road directly in our paths. Tire splash from cars and trucks drenched us. I was reminded of days in the swimming pool preparing for this trip, as I was so wet it seemed natural to turn my head to one side to breathe. Throughout the day we remained soaked with our riding clothes sopping wet, our shoes filled with water, and our fingers wrinkled like prunes. For as miserable as it should have been, for some reason the day didn't seem any more difficult than any others, only different. Cameras were stowed, so there weren't many pictures taken to document the day's journey.

Checking out the map above, you can see many, many different ways to get from St. Francisville to Franklinton; as we turned here and turned there, stopping often at SAG stops, the turns and stops helped to keep our minds focused on our objectives rather than our miseries. The countryside was lovely - wet, but lovely - the road surfaces were relatively level and smooth; and the wind was at our backs. All in all it was a memorable day, made more so by the flat I had that Linda and I changed in the pouring rain. Bubba promised us an adventure ,and we sure were getting it today.

Cuppa Java, Anyone?

Our first stop was in Clinton, at a Valero Gas Station, where Coasters were gathering to get out of the rain. The station was well-stocked with hot chocolate, coffee, and power bars, which those of us there consumed as we dripped water all over the place. Since I wasn't taking many pictures in the rain, I've included some that Ed took of an ad exec's approach to power advertising. These ads weren't at the Valero, but it captured the mood of the day. Power down a coffee, baby, you can sleep when you're dead.

Clinton is a delightful little town with a rich history portrayed in the architecture of its many small buildings dating to Civil War times. Linda had a letter to mail, so she turned down a

Note it's a Woman

side road, following a sign to the local post office. Since we were riding together today, I waited for her, sipping my hot chocolate (I was doing stupid things fast enough, thank you). I waited, and I waited, and I waited, and after about half an hour, I started to get worried that she had gotten into some trouble. Riding alone off the route indicated on our "route sheets" was a risky business since the SAG team wouldn't know where to look for you if you didn't show up at a designated stop. Just when I decided it was time to marshall a team to go look for her, she reappeared down the side road she had taken earlier. Apparently the post office indicated on the sign served several communities and was located way outside the center of Clinton.

Another stop we Coasters made was to visit Emanuel, an eighty-five year-old African-American retired paper mill worker, who sat on his front porch every year and welcomed Bubba's Pampered Pedalers as they cycled past. He wasn't in residence when Linda and I came by, but was there when Lisa and Jeff stopped. In Lisa's words:

We had the extreme privilege of meeting Immanuel, an 85-year-old man who lives on the corner of one of our turns near Clinton, LA. Bubba met him many years ago on his first cross country trip, and has been making it an annual stop ever since. Immanuel was born on Christmas Day, he worked in a saw mill his entire life where he lost most of his hearing, but he is very good at reading lips. I got to shake his hand and he held onto my wet hand extra long, and told us he would be praying for all of us to have a safe journey. He also said this was his favorite day of the year when he gets so much company. He lives in a very meager house, some might even call it a shack, but it is his home. Up until this past year, he shared it with his loyal dog Meatball. Sadly, Meatball died this year.

Bubba presented him with a box of left-over crawfish from our previous night's feast.

By the time most of us arrived at Hillcrest Baptist Church, where we were spending the night in their gym, rain had let up, and we all hoped the front had moved on by.

Pig's Lips?

I had never given much thought, never wanted to give much thought, to all the bits and pieces of pork left over after a pig has been slaughtered and the loins are neatly wrapped in plastic at the supermarket. I supposed most are somehow converted into dog food or find their way into cheap hot dogs, but lo, Bubba ran across a jar of pickled pigs lips at a local store. Just the idea of slicing the lips off a dead pig gives me the willies, but pickling them for future consumption at a picnic was beyond my imagination.

After dinner, Bubba brought out his jar and offered five dollars to anyone who would eat a lip, upper lip or lower lip, it didn't matter. Anyone crazy enough to ride across America ought to be crazy enough to eat a pickled pig's lip, right? and, sure enough, Larry won the five dollars to whoops and cheers from his fellow Coasters as he chewed off bite after bite declaring they weren't "all that bad." Adam, one of the Wolfpack, then ate one in anticipation of earning another five dollars offered by his Wolfpack comrades.

Things then got a little out of hand when the Wolfpack offered up twenty-five dollars to any one of their members who would drink the pint or so of pickling medium left in the jar. Sure enough, Adam took the bait and drank down the whole jar. Later (actually almost right away), he was video taped throwing up the whole mess on the church lawn and presumably didn't get the promised prize, as part of the deal was to keep the contents down. It's just as well he did throw it all up, as he might not have survived the night. Ah, the invincibility of youth!

Roadside pickup today was a **Child's Bike Seat**

April 15 - Day 40

Franklinton LA to Poplarville MS
45 Miles

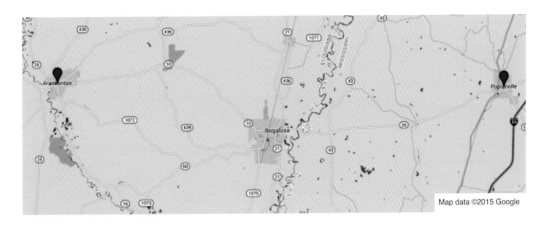

Map data ©2015 Google

Birthplace of America's Music?

Fog descended on Franklinton on this day and enveloped us Coasters for our first twenty miles. The sun finally began to clear the fog as we crossed the Pearl River separating Louisiana from Mississippi, and with that crossing we entered our sixth state. The welcome sign indicated that Mississippi was the birthplace of America's music. Did you know that? I certainly didn't know that, and wondered who gets to decide such historic gems. Would Tennessee concur?

The first SAG stop was at a wonderful Mississippi country restaurant, run by a lady who had been through Katrina in New Orleans and wanted no part of living that close to the coast again. Feeling well rested from a good night's sleep and in a particularly good mood, I had two dishes of strawberry ice cream at ten in the morning. From this stop, I remember biking through some of the most beautiful rural country in America.

One of the hazards of riding through rural countryside is the prevalence of pet dogs. There must be something about the sound of a bicycle that sets dogs off, because they start barking long before you get to them, and continue barking long after you're gone, even though you never see them. The hazards arise when those pet dogs are free to roam the countryside, go spastic at the sound of a bicycle on the road, and give chase. My solution at the beginning of the trip was to put a handful of dog biscuits in my jersey pocket, my thought being to throw a dog biscuit down if the dog got close enough to bite me. I never saw a dog as long as I had biscuits in my jersey and soon gave up carrying them. Of course as soon as I stopped carrying the biscuits, dogs began to appear, so my attention then turned to outrunning them wishing, all the while that I had a kept my dog biscuits. Once a dog encounter was successfully outrun, I usually spent some creative energy dreaming up ways to outfit my bike with a bulb filled with the ammonia connected to tubes running down to my feet, so when I squeezed the bulb ammonia would shoot the dog in the face. This is not a very Buddha-like use of one's imagination, but dogs are a real hazard when riding a bike. Bless Lisa for reminding us it wasn't the dogs who should suffer for only doing what they do naturally. It really was the owner's responsibility to keep their dogs restrained.

I had to admire Dan who growled, whistled, and snapped more ferociously than the dog, and if the dog didn't stop, he would whirl his bike around and start chasing the dog back to its house. Dan was a wonderful, unassuming sort who would then stop to talk to the dog's owners, eventually convincing most of them to keep the dogs inside until all us Coasters had passed. His stories of these discussions were always amusing, as some people were belligerent; some confessed they had no control over their dogs; and some were apologetic and immediately chained their dogs up. Me? I'd be worried I'd get shot by an irate homeowner as I invaded his property, so I just pedaled as fast as my legs could manage. I tried Dan's technique once on a small yappy dog, riding my bike right at him and barking like an idiot when the small dog's buddy, a huge pit bull, came out from behind a bush to defend his mate. I got out of there fast, resolving to never try anything that stupid again. I must have had too much coffee at breakfast. One dog actually ran across the road right in front of a pickup to attack Colleen and Randy on their tandem. He got greased by the truck and poor Colleen, a gentle animal lover, took it upon herself to go tell the owner how sad she was about the accident.

Ferocious Blue and Gold Wildcats

It was a short day, only forty-four miles, to Poplarville, Mississippi, home of the Pearl River Community College Wildcats. It was here at the college where the strongest gust from Hurricane Katrina was recorded at one hundred thirty-five miles per hour. I stopped first at the Poplarville Chamber of Commerce. They had posted a sign welcoming us Coasters to the town, a small community of only 3,000 people, and they gave us all a bag of goodies prepared by local merchants. Included in the bag was a brochure welcoming us back for a vacation stay.

As I pedaled down Main Street, I passed the Pearl River County courthouse. This one wasn't quite as imposing as the courthouses in Texas and Louisiana, but the statue in front of the courthouse caught my eye. It was a tribute to war heroes; - "Confederate Solders," "WW I Solders," and the "Devoted Women" who ran the farms while their men were off at war. The inscription under the Confederate soldier was, "To the men who wore gray and were faithful to the end." The idea of an independent southern

Pearl River County Courthouse

nation certainly has deep roots in Mississippi as it does across the whole South. As I write this, there is a furor over the Confederate Flag being a symbol of a racism that just won't die in the good old US of A, and I have to admit, whenever I see the flag I immediately associate it with slavery. That's a Confederate Flag you can barely see flying on the flagpole in front of the courthouse. Hopefully it will soon be a thing of the past, relegated to its rightful place in a museum.

It being a short day of only forty-five miles, I arrived in Poplarville in time for lunch at Scooters, famous for "Po-boys", a variety of sub made with pulled beef on a French roll. They're very good, and I recommend them highly, provided you have an ample supply of paper napkins to wipe the drippings off your elbows. The good mood that had given rise to my overdose of ice cream in the morning was now buoyed by the delicious Po-boy to the extent that I stopped at a Vietnamese nail shop and got the first pedicure of my life. Imagine, a Vietnamese nail shop in Poplarville, Mississippi? The pedicurist, who actually was Chinese, not Vietnamese, soaked my feet, rubbed my feet, cut my toenails, sanded my heels, and, yes, painted my toenails blue. When she pulled out the bottle of clear lacquer to paint my nails, I stopped her and indicated I wanted them colored. Eddy, a Coaster from Alabama, proudly displayed his maroon toenails as he walked around in his flip-flops, and I thought it

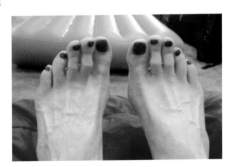

Twinkle Toes

would be fun to join him with a similar frivolity. The pedicurist gave me a shocked expression, hesitated for a moment, and then her face lit up and she howled,

"You want look like woman, ha, ha, ha, ha, ha, ha, ha?"

Once I recovered my composure from her verbal onslaught, I reassured her I wanted them painted blue, and so she did my bidding while every now and then, glancing at me sideways and shaking her head. I always feel sad for displaced persons, as I have lived for years overseas, and I know how hard it is to make a living and try to fit in as a foreigner in another culture. The fact is, you never do fit in, and your only hope is that your children will.

Bubba arranged for us Coasters to stay in the Poplarville Hurricane Shelter, a sturdy building constructed in response to the misery inflicted by hurricane Katrina upon the residents of the Mississippi Gulf Coast. What none of us knew about hurricane shelters, including Bubba who set this up, was that lights in hurricane shelters cannot be turned off. It does make sense to keep everything visible when hundreds of displaced, often destitute people are all crammed in together during an emergency. As a result of this government regulation, when lights-out time came at nine, they couldn't be turned out. It's interesting how much more difficult it is to sleep with lights on, but many of us had eye masks and I had a bandana I pulled down over my eyes. Someone mentioned that he saw Linda sitting up reading most of the night.

Roadside pickup today was a **Green Dress**

April 16 - Day 16

Poplarville to Ocean Springs
68 Miles

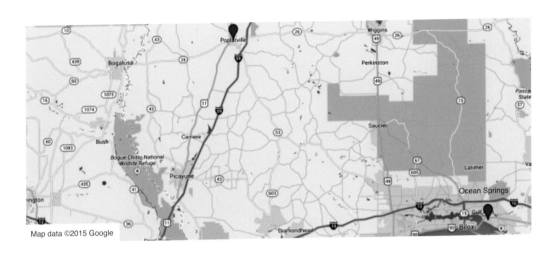

Map data ©2015 Google

John Welcoming Us to the SAG Stop

The forecast was for rain and more rain, and the NOAA radar showed the same line of storms that had been tailing us all week still out in the Gulf of Mexico and still waiting to pounce. Once again, we Coasters dodged the rain bullet and made it to Ocean Springs six hours later with nary a drop falling from the roiling, grey, overcast skies. The humidity was high and my glasses fogged, so I rode with them perched on the end of my nose as I squinted over the top, hoping a bee wouldn't get me in the eye. The first SAG stop was at a transformer station, and in the picture is John checking people off as they arrive. There were absolutely no restaurants along the route anywhere.

Fog also tended to diffuse my ability to discern details along the route, and I very foolishly relied on my rear view mirror to check on overtaking traffic during a left turn that I had to make across two lanes of highway. I looked in my mirror, saw nothing was coming (it was but I didn't see it), and headed out across the two lanes into the separate left turn lane. I was almost there when a car I hadn't seen appeared in that left turn lane so I stayed in the highway's fast lane until the car made its left turn. All of a sudden, I heard a vehicle behind me approaching fast, and without knowing where the fast approaching vehicle might be, I decided to get off the road as soon as possible and moved over into the right hand lane. I was in the middle of the slow lane headed for the shoulder when a pickup going at least seventy missed me by no more than a couple of inches. He had moved over to the slow lane to avoid me in the fast lane when I heard him, and then I moved over directly in front of him. Fortunately for the both of us he had good reflexes and was able to swerve in the nick of time. Had he not done so, I would have been killed. I think that's the closest I've ever come in my life.

Our route was all back roads this day offering a full spectrum of deep South poverty and deep South wealth. After my flirt with death, Linda and I traveled down a classy country road past horse properties, and we stopped to photograph one with an amazing entrance guarded by two huge black horse statues. The entrance alone was worth more than most

Linda at the Gates

of the houses we passed getting there. After I took the photo, the gates started to open slowly and a snazzy Porsche slipped out of the estate, driven by an even snazzier looking young lady.

Ramsey Creak Baptist Mission

The year prior Bubba had made contact with the Ramsey Creak Baptist Mission Church in Saucier, MS, and they agreed to make lunch for everyone. These four lovely ladies fed us sandwiches, potato salad, and granola bars and chatted with us about their support of overseas Christian missions. This they did from their little town in rural Mississippi, truly a noble calling, and they made no effort to

Ramsey Creek
BAPTIST CHURCH

IT HELPS TO REMEMBER
THAT GOD IS IN CONTROL
OF MY DAY--NOT ME.
WELCOME CYCLISTS !

And What a Welcome it Was

solicit funds or support from us Coasters. It was a very generous of them to simply do unto others. The marquee declaring their faith in the Almighty made a deep impression on me after surviving the closest brush with death I'd ever experienced in my life, and gave me pause to think about what I might have been saved for. I'm not particularly religious and don't necessarily sign up to the notion that a great being out there has plans for me, but something stirred in my soul when I saw that marquee and left me thinking about what I might set out to do when I returned from my Coast-to-Coast adventure.

We had a masseuse, Margie, along with the tour who worked as an independent contractor and went with us from campsite to campsite setting up her table and doing her thing rubbing sore muscles. She charged a dollar a minute, and much to my complete astonishment, her appointment book was always full; you had to book your massage days in advance to get one. Margie was a delightful sprite of a lady, but I had had massages in the past, and they had never done much for me. The last thing I want when my muscles ache is for someone to mash them into my bones. I'm sure it feels good when they stop, but then why ask them to do it in the first place? She was convinced she could relieve my aches and pains and told me, in a mocking voice on many occasions, that she couldn't wait to get her hands on me. I called her was "Never Never," since there was no way I was going to spend a dollar a minute to feel worse than I already did. She vowed to give everyone on the tour a massage, and I think I was her only holdout.

Margie

Our stop for the night was at a Motel 6 in Ocean Springs, named for mineral springs in the area reputed to have healing properties. The town went through several name changes throughout its history as it changed hands from French, to English, to Spanish, and finally to American. It was first called Fort Maurepas by Pierre Le Moyne d'Iberville during the reign of Louis XIV, who authorized its establishment in order to halt Spanish encroachment into French territory. The name was changed to Old Biloxi when the French were ousted from the area, and stayed Old Biloxi until, in 1854, an enterprising medical practitioner opened a hotel in town and called it the Ocean Springs Hotel. He pitched the local mineral spring's healing properties so well that the town became a popular destination for those with incurable ailments. The local residents, benefiting from the flood of dollars flowing to the area, changed the name of the town to Ocean Springs, a name more easily recognizable to those seeking the spring's curative properties.

Dining Room at Motel 6

We arrived in Ocean Springs in the early afternoon with a massive thunderstorm cell sitting directly to the west. It hit after dinner, which was a good thing, as Serge had set up the dinner tables in the motel parking lot and dinner was over just as the storm moved in.

This was the night Woody decided to leave the tour. He's the one who fell on the Atchafalaya Swamp bypass road, a spill we all later realized was caused by the diminished vision in his left eye. I really liked Woody for his calm demeanor and dry sense of humor.

Roadside pickup today **Two Plastic Doll's Arms**

Ocean Springs MS to Dauphin Island AL
82 Miles

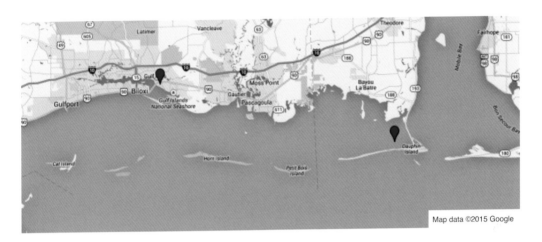

Map data ©2015 Google

The big storm off to our west hit overnight after I had turned in, and by morning the skies were clearing and most of the ugly weather was moving to the east. Nevertheless, it was very humid, and water-laden clouds hung low as we Coasters left the hotel. The morning was all more of the same beautifully-paved narrow roads, luscious green pastures, and pickups boiling past us on blind corners. Not having a shoulder on which to ride sure kept me on my toes. On this lovely morning, Monica had stopped to take a picture and got grazed by car driving too close. She was OK, but it was another grim reminder that this biking activity isn't without its risks.

Why Did the Turtle Cross the Road?

It always pained me to see turtles squished along the side of the road, a pain far more intense than the pain I felt when I saw squished armadillos, which, truth be told, wasn't all that much. So whenever I saw one of these gentle creatures trying to make its lumbering way to the other side of the road, I stopped and ushered it along its way. I'd been told by those who know about such things, that I should always put the turtle on the side of the road to which it is headed and never put it back where it came from, as it will only try to cross again. That same informed naturalist never did explain to me why a turtle is tempted to cross a road in the first place. Are turtles just like the rest of us, never satisfied with what they have but always wanting more, more, more? There goes my wandering, wondering restless brain.

Sam, Linda, and Tom in Alabama

Our passage into Alabama was a statement of fact as opposed to a warm welcome, but Tom, Linda, and I stopped to record our progress. It was the seventh state we'd entered since we started the trek, and I know I was feeling a bit glum that our great adventure was soon to be over.

Onward, the three of us biked through the lush countryside saving turtles until we arrived at Bayou La Batre, an early French settlement on the coast originally given the rather romantic name of "Riviere D'Erbane." Then the French built a coastal battery on the spot and renamed the town "Bayou La Batre" or, in English, "Bayou of the Battery," not very romantic, but that's the military for you. The Spanish then wrested the land from the French and the Americans wrested it from the Spanish, but nobody bothered to change the name.

All cyclists worried about hitting some obstacle in the road causing a spill, and whether it was a hole, a pavement separation, or a piece of trash, we were always on the lookout for something that would cause us to lose our balance. Drainage grates can pose a danger if they have sunk below the level of the pavement, but most are designed such

Bayou La Batre

that bicycles can travel over them without incident. In Bayou La Batre, however, the drainage grates were designed like oven grills with longitudinal bars but no lateral bars. Sure enough on Bubba's 2014 C2C, the front wheel of one of the riders slipped down into one of the grates causing the bike to stop short, throwing the rider over the handlebars. She fractured her collar bone. Bubba warned us of this danger along our route and told us he had made it a point to call the town attorney and mention the potential liability. Sure enough, as we passed through Bayou La Batre we saw that the grates had cross pieces welded on to prevent the recurrence of an accident. I rode around the grates just to be on the safe side.

Bayou La Batre is a fishing village whose chamber of commerce call it the "Seafood Capital of Alabama" for all its shrimp processing operations. In addition to shrimp processing, it is home to many shrimp boats who provide the processing plants with their catch. Boat building and maintenance is also an industry pursued in the port. The town received some note when it was featured in the film "Forrest Gump" as he pursued his shrimping enterprise. Also, a square rigged ship was built there to be used in the filming of "Pirates of the Caribbean." The town was hit especially hard by Hurricane Katrina with a sixteen foot storm surge that relocated many of the area shrimp boats inland. I checked the Internet for information about the impact of Katrina on Bayou La Batre and found the NOAA photo featured on the next page. Bayou La Batre's sister city, Santa Monica in California, came to the rescue of the smaller shrimp boats with the loan of truck mounted cranes capable of raising them off the land and transporting them back to the water. The larger shrimp boats, well, many of them are still sitting inland where they were washed up. The *Caribbean Clipper* cargo ship in the photo was lifted back in the water with a really, really big crane.

Bubba had worked me into a frenzy of anticipation the previous evening describing our lunch break this day at Preacher's BBQ, a restaurant famous for the best fried oysters in

Impact of Hurricane Katrina*

Bayou La Batre. Sadly, it had gone out of business since the 2014 C2C had come through, so we ate at McDonalds. When you're burning up close to 4000 calories a day, you don't feel so guilty putting away a double quarter-pounder with cheese, large fries, and a vanilla shake. I took the opportunity to take a photo of four of our group powering down their mega calorie meals. Bubba is in the easy chair, the only easy chair I've ever seen in a McDonald's restaurant. He looks relaxed and calm here, but I'm sure his mind was spinning with how he would deal with the latest unforeseen problem. Every day

Joe, Tom, John, and Cecil

Bubba Relaxing

brings a new challenge, from a bike accident to a cancelled reservation, and he was a master at handling them all with great success - never, ever, letting his worries carry over to his Coasters. He is a very special guy.

From Bayou La Batre, we crossed over the Intra-coastal Waterway bridge to Dauphin Island, named during those days when the French occupied all these coastal lands. Early explorations by the French who were looking for a deep water port on the island unearthed huge piles of skeletons, so the island was originally named "Massacre Island." It was never determined for sure how all the people died, and there were so many skeletons it had been posited that the island served as a burial ground rather than a massacre site. The French eventually renamed the island "Dauphin" to honor the heir to the French throne, and the name has stuck through all its nationality changes.

Sam Entering Dauphin Island

Mother Goose Condos

There were some wonderful architectural firsts on entry to the island, and the row of condominiums looking like a picture out of Mother Goose was a treat worthy of a photo. I can't imagine what the insides of these condos look like, but they certainly would define an interesting minimalist idea in living space. I almost expected them all to suddenly start dancing about as cartoon characters, while blinking their upstairs windows and talking through their open front doors.

We Coasters spent the night in the Dauphin Island Park and Beach where we'd spend another most welcome rest day.

Roadside pickup today was a **Child's Life Vest**

*NOAA Photo

April 18 - Day 43

Dauphin Island
Rest Day

Dauphin Island Park and Beach is a 155-acre campground with a large community center, ample showers, and a general store stocked with sufficient ice cream to keep us all well supplied. The park was within walking distance of an Audubon bird sanctuary, a US Coast Guard station, and Fort Gaines, a Confederate fort built to defend Mobile Bay against Union attackers. The island is a fourteen-mile long "barrier island," so called as it is supposed to form a barrier between the open ocean and the mainland. It is little more than a large sand spit and certainly vulnerable to any hurricanes headed its way. The island provided little barrier security, as Katrina washed over it in 2005, doing extensive damage to the Alabama shoreline. I slept soundly secure in the knowledge that few hurricanes ever enter the Gulf of Mexico in April.

More cloudy skies greeted us in the morning and it was hard to believe that the front along the gulf coast hadn't moved in ten days. As soon as the weather showed any signs of lifting, another band of showers showed up on the radar.

Summer Cottage?

Tom and I braved the elements this day and decided to bike to the end of the island to see what we could see. This part of America is affectionately referred to as the "Redneck Riviera," where tourists flock during the summer months to bask on the beach and stay in houses built on stilts designed to protect them from storm surge water damage. The design specifications for these stilts were all modified after Katrina cleaned off the island in 2005. The summer cottage of yore being a relatively small, fragile structure with few amenities has morphed into a gigantic summer home replete with central air conditioning, Le Cornue kitchens, and whirlpool baths. Tom and I saw many of these magnificent summer homes, some finished and many more under construction, as we cycled west along the island. It will be interesting to see how many of them survive the next hundred year storm. Some of these homes were selling for half a million dollars. There is a rumor that the only insurance you can get for these homes is government sponsored, a program wisely putting your hard-earned tax dollars to work.

On the way back from our junket to the west it started to rain, and by the time Tom and I reached the campground it was pouring. In we headed to the community center, where several of the ladies were working on a 1000-piece picture puzzle. The goal was to finish the puzzle in our one rest day, so activity around the table was electric in its intensity.

Marla, Frances, Beth, Judy, and Linda

Toward dinner time, there was a cry of exaltation when the last piece was put in, and everybody stood back, beaming with the pride that comes with success. The community center had a library well stocked with books and puzzles that kept growing with its take-one-leave-one philosophy, where many left more than they took.

The park sat adjacent to Fort Gaines, a restored Civil War fort designed to blast attacking ships out of the water before they could enter Mobile Bay. Another fort, Fort Morgan, sat on the other side of the entrance to the bay, and these two forts were in a high state of alert when Admiral Farragut was given the order to seize Mobile during the Civil War. He was famous for his command, "Damn the torpedoes, full speed ahead." A torpedo in those days was what we now call a mine, and he issued the orders to an ironclad

gunship captain, concerned that his vessel might hit one. Subsequent to the famous command, the gunship actually hit a torpedo and sank, fully justifying its captain's concern. History, however, credited Farragut with noble courage in the face of grave danger, but hey, it wasn't his ship that was in danger, what did he care? (It's easy to be a philanthropist with someone else's money). The sinking, however, cleared the way for the admiral's attack on Mobile, the success of which closed the port to Confederate trade, thereby helping to end the war. Both Fort Gaines and Fort Morgan had all their guns pointed toward the mouth of the bay, so once Farragut got through the mouth, he was home free.

Damn Those Torpedoes

The skies cleared by afternoon, so Joe, Linda, Tom, and I headed out to visit the various sights at the east end of the island, starting with the park general store. Here we relieved them of their stash of ice cream sandwiches, and we then ambled over to Fort Gaines. They wanted eight dollars apiece to walk around and look at stone battlements we'd already seen at other places many times before, so we stayed outside and took pictures. Outside the fort there were many cannons dotting the perimeter pointing in the right direction toward the bay rather than away from it. Better late than never I always say.

Beam Me Up, Katrina

The Estuarium was an interesting boardwalk around some sand dunes explaining the cause and effects of weathering, particularly the effects of hurricanes. There was even a hurricane chamber simulating the wind from a hurricane, and Joe drew the short straw to feel the effects. We were hoping the wind would tear his clothes off, but all it did was muss his hair a bit. Some hurricane. We were all disappointed. The Estuarium also exhibited the damage done by human interaction with natural processes as humans dump garbage in the seas and build along unprotected coastlines. It's sad that we humans know what we are doing to destroy our planet, but we can't muster the will to do anything about it. I've felt for some time that it takes an episode of enormous destructiveness to set the wheels of progress in motion to institute change. I do wonder if the episode that will inspire humans to do something about our selfish tendencies won't come too late and be so enormously destructive that it destroys humanity in the process.

Our agenda for April 19 had us boarding the ferry for Fort Morgan to take us to the other end of the mouth of the bay. The forecast was for more rain. I stayed hopeful, but had I known what we were in for I might not have slept as well as I did.

April 19 - Day 44

Dauphin Island AL to Milton FL
85 Miles

Pastor Ed Gillette

This being Sunday, Ed conducted his fifteen-minute devotions before breakfast. As I mentioned previously, Ed was a man of great faith who had spent his life doing good works in the name of that faith. He was quite tolerant of my differing perspective on the concept of God, and we had some interesting discussions about that differing perspective. One such discussion focused on the idea of "original sin", and Ed listened attentively as I explained my dismay at the impression we are all born somehow bad because Adam disobeyed God and ate the apple. I mean, after all, it was Adam who disobeyed God - why am I held responsible for his screw up? Most of us have a hard enough time developing a positive self image, and to start off life with the idea we are bad to begin with just isn't very helpful. The corollary idea that all this original sin can be washed away with baptism and actual sin forgiven by confession has never sat very well with me.

While in Richards, TX during a rest day, I sat with Ed on a bench swing and gave him my Buddhist approach on the subjects of original sin, forgiveness, and eternal life. On the subject of original sin, I explained that if the idea were couched in terms that all humans possess self-destructive tendencies, - namely greed, hatred, and delusion - then the idea of original sin would make more sense. Since these tendencies exist in all human beings, we shouldn't feel shame or embarrassment for exhibiting them, but should be counseled in ways to overcome them. Washing in holy water or confessing to a priest wouldn't overcome them, but living a life of generosity, loving kindness, and seeing the world as it is, would help. I then broached the subject of the parallels that existed between the Christian concept of eternal life in Heaven and the Buddhist concept of eternal life through reincarnation. Ed listened, smiled, and told me he thought these interpretations were excellent.

Well, it finally caught up with Bubba's Pampered Pedalers - the rain that is. At six a.m. it was pouring as everybody scrambled to get their gear packed and ready for the trucks. The rain turned the campsite into a lake several inches deep in places, and many tent bottoms weren't waterproof, so bags left in the tents were soaked when loaded for transit. I waded around in my flip flops until it was time to depart, hoping to avoid having to ride with wet shoes and socks. The rain did let up after breakfast, and I took heart that we Coasters might have dodged another bullet.

We were advised to get to the ferry at seven-thirty to be ready for an eight-o'clock departure, so all us Coasters gathered in front of the ferry, like a group of kindergartners all holding hands waiting to cross the road, and we waited, all of us except Bruce. I'm not sure what Bruce was up to at the end of the pier, but he suddenly let out a haunting, unnerving wail. It seemed he had leaned over the pier to look at something in the water when his iPhone slid out of his shirt pocket and went *plunk* into the briny deep. Several efforts were made to retrieve it with sticks and brooms, including an effort by Linda, who volunteered to wade out to the point of entry, but all these efforts proved fruitless. Linda aborted her effort after she took three steps into the water (each one sinking her eighteen inches deeper), and realized the fourth step might just put the water over her head. Bruce kept his cool and philosophized about how there was no real harm done, as iPhones can always be replaced. This really was an amazing group of psychologically well balanced individuals.

Just as we were all telling Bruce how unfortunate it was for him to lose his cell phone (while secretly thanking our lucky stars it was him and not us); a thunderclap ripped

Singing In the Rain . . . Yeah Right!

through the humid miasma that had settled over the island announcing another forthcoming deluge. And what a deluge it was. There we all were in our rain gear at seven-thirty huddled en masse along the dock with our shoes and socks getting soaked. The captain of the ferry didn't want to leave in such a torrent, so we all stood around like yellow penguins until, until... Marla, bless her heart, lifted everyone spirits by bursting out with "Singing in the Rain" as she danced through the puddles with the lightness and grace of Gene Kelly.

We were a pretty sad group of drowned rats when the ferry finally started loading about eight-thirty during a break in the rain.

On the Ferry to Fort Morgan

As I looked out across the bay from the ferry pier, I could just make out what looked like platforms dedicated to petroleum production. From the shore it was hard to tell if they were drilling platforms or production platforms, however the ferry brought us close enough to one of them during our crossing that I could see there was a derrick on one from which the wells would have been drilled. There was a gas flare boom on the other platform where the facilities to process the production would have been located. This trip reminded me of my days working on the oil production platforms with Shell Oil company so many years ago. I learned later that the production from this field was all natural gas.

Gas Production in Mobile Bay

The ferry reached Fort Morgan, the other fort with guns still pointing the wrong way, and we Coasters headed down a new road built across the sand spit more or less at sea level. As the road dipped, we rode through puddles of water, some four inches deep, and squirmed and wiggled as water rooster-tailed up our riding shorts. The amount of building going on along the coast was breathtaking, with small houses on stilts, large houses on stilts, and thirty-story luxury high rises on stilts. As I mentioned, locals call this area the "Redneck Riviera" though I doubt there are many folks we in the northeast think of as "redneck" who could afford any of these places.

Once past the dunes, we crossed into Florida, our eighth and last state. To the left is a picture of John standing alongside his recumbent bike, "Big Blue."

John and "Big Blue," His Bike

Linda Waving for a Whistle

Florida was a rare treat. The pavement was mostly new, every road had a bike lane, and the wind was at our backs, so Linda and I were able to pedal merrily along in a blissful state.

The route was carefully mapped by Bubba so that we'd avoid Pensacola traffic, but Linda and I took a wrong turn and cycled right down through the middle of town. We had to stop at a Ramada Inn to get pointed in the right direction, and even then we managed a couple more wrong turns and an unscheduled stop at a railroad crossing. Look carefully and you'll see Linda waving at the engineer hoping he would acknowledge her attentions with a whistle. He didn't.

The road north out of Pensacola took us along the western shore of Escambia Bay, where Linda and I encountered sights that were a delight for our traveling eyes. The first of these was a Dairy Queen. No dedicated cyclist ever passes up a Dairy Queen, and this one was no exception. Once sated on root beer floats and giant soft ice cream cones, we set out looking for an oddly Asian-looking residence that Bubba had highlighted on our route sheets. Bubba told us he had approached the house on several occasions to find

Unique Residence on Escambia Bay

out who owned it, what it was all about, and whether his Coasters might take a guided tour. No one ever answered the door, much to his disappointment, and ours as well. It looked like an Indian palace, and the grounds seemed to be dedicated to some form of Hindu or Buddhist worship. Unfortunately, it appeared to be in a state of benign neglect with garden statuary all tipping one way or the other.

On Linda and I biked, to Milton, a town of 7,000 residents established in support of the lumber industry. Benjamin Jernigan built a saw mill there around 1828. and for while the slowly growing community was called Jernigan's Landing. Everybody kept calling it the "mill town," and eventually the name "Milton" stuck. The Confederate army burned the town to the ground, including the sawmill, during the war to keep it from falling into Union hands. Most of the inhabitants fled to Alabama once their houses and livelihoods had disappeared, thanks to the actions of their own people. The chimney from the sawmill is still standing in a park dedicated to the memory of the war. There just isn't much one can say about war that doesn't include human tragedy.

Chimney of Jernigan's Mill

Linda liked to ride in front, and I was following her on our last stretch to Milton when I came upon a black, lady's dress-up shoe on the side of the road she had overlooked. I thought she might like it for her Roadside Virgin, so I sped up and asked her if she was interested. She said she had enough shoes and didn't need any more. When I told her it was adorned with sequins, she lit up like a roman candle - "SEQUINS!" she fairly yelled, "of course I want it," and so she went back and hung it on her handlebars. I went on ahead, and a quarter mile down the road I spied the other

Vince Camuto Dress Shoes

shoe, which she picked up and hung with the first. The shoes were almost new, and later she Googled the name Vince Camuto stenciled on the inside sole, and there it was, a picture of the very shoe we had found with a list price of one hundred dollars. At the dinner announcements that night, we told the group about our roadside find and when Linda declared, "Who needs a man who can hunt and fish when there's one around who can find new shoes" the house came down. Amazingly enough, the shoes were Linda's size.

Isn't it wonderful be be alive?

We stayed at a KOA (Campgrounds of America) campground this night and, while the air was warm and humid, there was no sign of rain. I did note there was a another huge storm hovering in the Gulf of Mexico, so who knew what we'd be up against on the morrow.

Roadside pickup today was a **Pair of Vince Camuto Dress Shoes**

April 20 - Day 45

Milton to Defuniak Springs
55 Miles

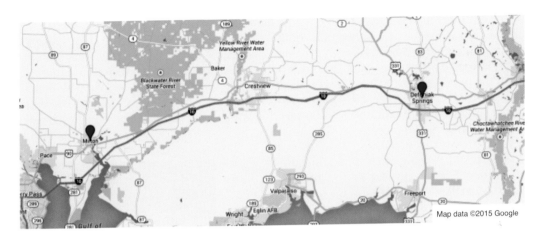

Map data ©2015 Google

After going to bed under clear skies and certain that the rest of our voyage would be held under the Florida sun, we awoke to clouds and soaked earth. That big storm we'd seen on radar the day before was still hovering, so most Coasters outfitted themselves with rain gear, expecting the worst.

Incredible as it seemed to all of us, Linda was the only rider without having had a flat tire. Tom, her brother, whispered to me I should sneak out to her bike in the middle of the night and let the air out of one tire. Then we'd all have a good laugh at breakfast. Brothers are so mean, but not so mean he would do it himself. It reminded me of Admiral Farragut, "Damn the consequences, Sam, go let the air out of her tire." We didn't have to pull any such stunt, as she was the first to get a flat once we got underway. Of course, she did it right where a SAG truck was parked, so all she had to do was snap her fingers, and it was repaired by Murph, who had replaced Chandler as our resident bicycle mechanic.

Linda's First and Only Flat Tire

There were now forty-one riders in our group, four having dropped out for one reason or another, and, one, Bill, having joined us at Dauphin Island after dropping out of the 2014 C2C when his wife was in an auto accident. Bill got off to a tough start, having four flats the first day out as we rode into Milton. Bill had the same problem telling if he had a flat that I did. It is possible to ride with a flat tire, especially if the cyclist is riding fast, as the only sensation felt is a certain squiggly action from your bike. The slower you go the more squiggly your bike would become. Bill changed three of his four flats but was so frustrated by the time he got the fourth one he kept riding, believing he could manage until the next SAG stop. Unfortunately the squiggly bike bit him and he lost his balance, fell, and did something to his shoulder requiring ice all night. Cecil had had the most flats and each night at dinner he announced how many he had had that day. So far he'd had fourteen. I'd had four.

At one point, we saw an example of chain saw art. The three figures cut out of the tree trunk look something like cats, but it's a bit hard to tell. The letters on the tree trunk were DCD, but nobody knew what that meant.

And then, what state would be complete without a "Niceville?" I could imagine a group of town fathers sitting around trying to come up with a name for a town.

"How about Niceville?" one offers, "Everyone who lives here is pretty nice."

"Niceville, are you nuts?" another rages, "Nobody names a town Niceville. We need a honking, macho name like Tombstone."

"I don't know," third pipes up, "I kind of like Niceville, why don't we put it up for vote?"

Tree Sculpture

Oh Really?

So much for my imagination. It seems the town was originally called Boggy, a name that stuck from 1868 until 1910 when for some unknown reason (to me), the town fathers decided to change it. The task of choosing a name was given to the Postmaster's daughter, and her pick was Niceville. There is just something awfully sweet about that story, as I can see an eight-year old beaming with pride as the name she offered was chosen by the town fathers. "Mosses Head" was the next town over, and

I suppose I'd opt for "Niceville" over "Mosses Head" were it left up to me. We didn't actually go through Niceville, so I have no idea if it was nice. What I have found along our routes, though, is a country full of the nicest people one can possibly imagine. It certainly gave me a sense of what a great place America is.

Like Mushrooms After a Rain

I mentioned previously that in the poorer towns we passed through in the West, the three standout stores seemed to be a general store (liquor and guns), a gas station, and a dollar store. It's this dollar store phenomenon that attracted my attention on this, our forty-fifth day on the road. They were springing up like mushrooms after a heavy rain. I saw three in a row in one shopping center, Family Dollar, Dollar General, and The Dollar Store. Every town we went through then, and I mean EVERY town, had some version of a dollar store. There's one in Keene I went to once, and, sure enough, everything in the store cost a dollar. I can't get over thinking what they're all going to do if we get a wave of inflation. Motel 6 is now Motel 36, and I suppose the same will happen to these stores. I can envision the Family Five Dollar, Five Dollar General, and... well, you get the picture. They're adding one more plank in the Americana platform defining who we are as a nation of rabid consumers.

Our overnight was at the lovely Sunset King Lake Resort and RV park in Defuniak Springs, where we Coasters arrived after a relatively short day with, again, rain threatening but never falling. This resort appeared to be a landing spot for people in their sunset years who bought an RV, drove it to Florida, and planted it at Sunset King. I don't believe one could find a more cohesive and active community of seniors anywhere in America. Dinner was prepared for us by the residents and served in the resort community building. After dinner, Bubba announced that the ladies in the park had so impressed him with their quilted handiwork when he visited them in 2014, he asked if they could make quilted purses

Cyclist's Purse

with a cycling motif for the 2015 tour. They readily agreed to take on the project, provided Bubba would assure them we cyclists would buy all they could produce. Lo and behold, Bubba wheeled out fifty purses after dinner and begged us all to buy one so that he wouldn't have to honor his pledge to take them all. He expected eight or ten and, when he was presented with fifty, he could see his entire C2C budget blown. The purses, well designed with many inside pockets and extremely well made, were all immediately snapped up. For twenty dollars you couldn't go wrong. Linda bought four.

A large gazebo stood In the center of the park where we were entertained by a country western DJ who played all our old favorites as well as some I'd never heard of. He was set up to do Karaoke, but only Chandler had the nerve to sing for the group. He did an hysterical rendition of "Bad" that had us all cheering and yelling. Every cancer survivor in the group then sang a ballad together before turning the program over to the DJ who played favorites until the nine o'clock lights out.

Roadside pickup today was a **Net for Cleaning a Swimming Pool**

April 21 - Day 46

Defuniak Springs to Marianna
69 Miles

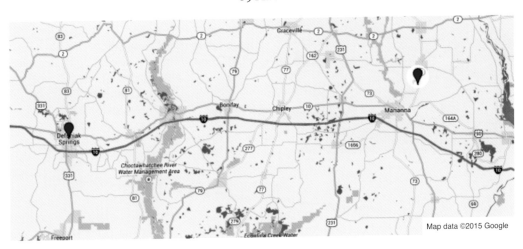

The Sunset King Lake Resort where we Coasters stayed wasn't exactly in Defuniak Springs. It was a couple of miles from the resort to the main road and then a couple of miles into Defuniak Springs down the main highway. We Coasters all headed out after a full breakfast, again prepared by the kind residents of the park. As soon as I left the park, I noticed a rhythmic vibration in my bike, an odd *nip, nip, nip* which seemed to be related to the speed I was traveling. After checking over both tires for high spots and finding nothing, I continued on, doing the best I could to block it out of my mind. The blocking seemed to work, as I was less aware of it as the day unfolded.

Defuniak Springs Public Library

The town of Defuniak Springs we rode through, with a current population of about 5000, was established during the late 1800s to support the railroad expansion of the Louisville and Nashville Railroad. It was named after Frederick Defuniak, Vice President of the company. There was a small lake in the center of town, Lake Defuniak, possibly the spring to which the town name refers, and a circular drive around the lake. The first building we encountered as we turned onto this circular drive was the oldest library in Florida, the Walton Defuniak Library, which was established in 1886. Interestingly enough, the oldest public

Sword Anyone?

library in the United States was created in Peterborough, NH in 1833, so it took fifty-three years for the idea to strike a resonant chord in Defuniak Springs, and it only did so because a group of ladies got together to make it happen. I wonder what these same ladies would think about our crew of lady Coasters? *You've come a long way baby!!* The library building is also the oldest building in Florida, built as a library and continuously operated as a library since it opened. I biked past the building, as I arrived before it opened, but John took a tour and photographed a large collection of swords adorning the walls. We humans do love our instruments of physical coercion, don't we?

Pedaling around the lake on Circle Drive, Linda and I encountered many beautiful homes before we headed out into the rural Florida countryside. The rides were getting easier and easier, due in part I'm sure to my physical conditioning, but made more so because the weather was warm and the smoothly-paved roads unraveled in front of us without radical elevation changes. Finally leaving chipseal pavement behind was such a blessed relief.

On the way to points east we went through the town of Ponce de Leon, a name I remember from junior high. Ponce de Leon was a Spanish conquistador who was appointed the first governor of Puerto Rico. Apparently he liked his job so much he never wanted to grow too old to do it, so off he plunged through the countryside to

At Last the Fountain of Youth

discover the Fountain of Youth. He failed to find the fountain, but he did find Florida, which he is responsible for naming. Florida, incidentally, was named Pascua Florida on Easter in 1513. It means "Flowering Easter" after Spain's "Feast of the Flowers." I wonder how long old Ponce waited after consuming a flagon of the waters in Defuniak Springs before he realized he was still batting zero in his quest to become young again.

On an interesting side note, one of Linda's friends, Skee, who was reading my daily blog of the C2C, saw my referral to Miss Marble, one of my seventh grade teachers responsible for my knowledge of the Gadsden Purchase. She emailed me asking where I had gone to junior high as she had had a Miss Marble in her seventh grade junior high as well. Small world, as we had both been to the same junior high in Weston,

Massachusetts, where Miss Marble had taught. Skee had been several years behind me, so we had never met, but what an amazing coincidence. Then, again, maybe there is no such thing as a coincidence. Food for thought.

Every town should be famous for something, and sure enough, the town of Caryville was famous for "worm fiddlin'." Now "worm fiddlin'," or "worm doodling," or "worm snoring" is a technique used by fisherpeople to bring worms to the surface of the ground where they can be harvested. There are several techniques to do this and all involve driving a stick or post into the ground and then making it vibrate like a fiddle string. Worms don't seem to appreciate the vibrating ground

You Really Have to be Kidding

and seek shelter from the racket above ground. Caryville has a "Fiddlin'" festival each year, and rumor has it that most of the winners are women.

At the entrance to the Arrowhead RV Park and Campground in Marianna, I, of sharp eye for the soft, cold and sweet, spotted a yoghurt shop right before the turn into the park. This occasioned a brief stop to quench my addiction, so I pulled in to indulge myself. This particular yoghurt shop adhered to the philosophy of self service without the client realizing what the product will cost until arriving at the checkout scales. I merrily picked the largest empty container available and began pulling handles to release the various flavors of yoghurt from the many machines around the shop until my container was mounded at the top with yoghurt. The shock of finding out that yoghurt sells for ten dollars a pound, and I had my cup filled with close to two pounds of the stuff, had me staring blankly at the cash register, unable to make eye contact with the cashier for fear of detecting a wry smile depicting an inner knowledge that he had snagged another sucker. Once I'd emptied my wallet, however, the yoghurt was most refreshing, made more so because I knew I had paid top dollar for it.

After my gluttony at the yoghurt shop, I proceeded to the RV park where we'd be camping for the night. When I think RV, I think Recreational Vehicles: pickup trucks towing Airstream trailers with canoes on top and mountain bikes strapped on behind. And campgrounds, well my imagination takes me to lush pastures bordering crystal clear alpine lakes, a level tent platform, an adjoining picnic table, and an accompanying barbecue pit.

Ahem!

Times have changed. Arrowhead RV Park certainly had it's share of RVs, but many could

no longer be classified as recreational, and some weren't even vehicular. I didn't see one Airstream - in fact I didn't see one small trailer towed by a modest SUV. What I saw were massive homes on wheels looking a lot like intercontinental busses, which, when parked, extended their sides to double the inside living space. Some monster RVs were towed by Cummins' Diesel-powered Ford F-350 tractors equipped with a fifth wheel, and some actually were busses, with built-in power

Immobile Home

plants and a captain's console in the bow. These, at least, were mobile allowing them to be classified as vehicles. Up the food chain were RVs that were once mobile, but which had remained stationary so long that they had grown skirts, maybe even roots. Finally I came upon a home, the one on the left, that had once been mobile but had now been in one spot for ten years. It took up two sites, one for the structure and one for the garden in front. After the Sunset Lake Resort, and now Arrowhead, it had finally become clear to me that while I had always thought of RV parks as transient stopovers, they were seen by many as permanent retirement communities.

And the campground part of Arrowhead, well, we tenters were certainly the most mobile of the entire population, and we'd all have to wait for another day to enjoy that crystal clear alpine lake. We were mashed together cheek by jowl right next to the main dirt road into the campground. I was a little worried about a pickup tooling into the park after its driver had downed a few, missing the turn, and plowing into a row of tents. Fortunately this never came to pass.

Like Peas in a Pod

This was to be our last night in the tents, and I was looking eagerly forward to less rustic accommodations.

Roadside pickup today was a **Baby Blanket**

April 22 - Day 47

Marianna to Tallahassee
75 Miles

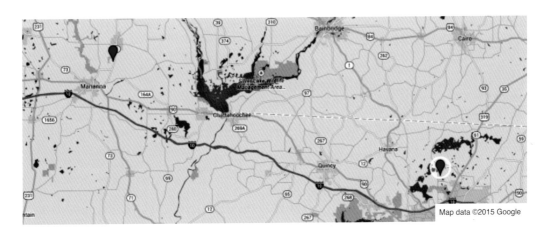

Map data ©2015 Google

After Chandler, our mechanic, had his accident, his duties were taken over by others on the tour. David, or Coach as he liked to be called, one of the recumbent riders, had served as the resident mechanic on other tours, and his knowledge of bicycles was extensive. You might recall that I started out the day before with an odd *nip, nip, nip* emanating from my machine, but I was not able to locate the source, I made it to Marianna without mishap. Before heading out on this particular morning, I decided to consult Coach and get a second opinion about my rear tire, with my diagnosis that it was nothing being somewhat suspect. Coach put my bike up on the rack, and after a few minutes of slowly turning my rear wheel he found a lump, not a big lump mind you, but a lump nonetheless. It appeared the tire cord was separating, and the prognosis was a sure flat at some juncture. Putting on a new tire seemed to be the best course of action.

Tom, Linda, and I had made all the recommended purchases of spare parts, so I selected one of the Continental Gator Hardshell road tires Tom had bought to the tune of roughly seventy dollars a tire. After struggling for half an hour to put it on, Chandler, who didn't any longer do the work but who served as a consultant to those who did, noticed a slit in the side. Apparently it was caused by a box knife while an employee was opening a shipment at the bike shop. *Rats!* Off came my wheel.

My next choice was a heavier touring tire I had bought for my Erie Canal ride over crushed gravel, but I had never used it, so I packed it along. I felt the heavier tread would make it less susceptible to the wires we picked up so often from retreads thrown off by eighteen-wheelers. After the usual half hour struggle to mount this tire, I put the wheel back on the bike and lo, it wouldn't turn. The thicker tread jammed up against the bike chainstays and wouldn't budge. *Rats!* Off came my wheel for the second time.

Anne had made breakfast early this day because it was going to be a long day, and Bubba thought it best if everyone got off to an early start. By the time I took my wheel off for the third time, the camp was clearing out, and I was one of the last left.

My third tire was borrowed from Chandler's stock, a used tire that would have to do until I could get a new one to replace it. A half hour later, it was on my bike and I was ready to go. By then the tents had all been taken down and packed into the Penske, breakfast had been eaten and tables cleared, and I was the last to leave the campsite. I don't like being last - a topic I maybe ought to have discussed with the two psychologists along on the tour. Feeling alone and forgotten, I pedaled at breakneck speed into the gathering Florida dawn down Route 90 hoping to catch up with someone, anyone, so I wouldn't be last.

It wasn't long before I spotted something along the route that I was sure Linda would treasure. I used clip in pedals, as did most of the cyclists on the tour, and as I slowed down to pick up the treasure, I automatically unclipped my right foot from the pedal. I always unclipped my right foot secure in the knowledge I would lean to the right when I finally stopped so I could put my right foot out. I was so intent on picking up what I saw on the side of the road that something happened, and my weight shifted to the left. In an instant I knew I was going to go down unless I could unclip my left foot fast enough, and alas, alack, I wasn't able to. Down I went on my left knee, tearing out the usual square inch of skin. Fortunately none of my comrades were there to witness the mishap, but now, not only was I last, but I was last and I hurt.

But, I put on a happy face and soldiered on. Then, as I was merrily whistling down the road, some sort of stinging insect hit me in the thigh with its stinger pointing right at me. It let loose a massive dose of formic acid that created shivers of pain radiating down my right leg and up my right side. My knee suddenly felt positively good by comparison. I'd heard stories of bee stings causing allergic reactions severe enough to kill people, and while I'd been stung by bees in the past, nothing had ever hurt so much or caused such an immediate reaction. I didn't know what it was that stung me so I didn't know what to expect, but I'm pretty sure it wasn't a honey bee as I'd been stung by them before without anywhere near such a violent impact to my nervous system. Accordingly, I stopped my bike as soon as I recovered from the shock, got off after unclipping my shoes, and sat by the side of the road waiting to die. After a few minutes the shivering stopped and, realizing I was probably going to survive, I returned to my journey, my trifecta of misery slowly receding under the pavement.

Riding through the Florida panhandle was delightful when you didn't encounter insects, but the delight was limited to excellent road surfaces, wide shoulders, unending green fields and forests, and few hills. There just weren't many photo ops that weren't repetitive. A good one I did encounter was the old Route 90 bridge across the Chattahoochee River. These old concrete arch bridges were so much more artistically appealing than steel truss bridges. I do wish our public works departments paid more attention to beauty over utility, and of course many do. I think the new suspension bridges, with their tall towers and radiating cables, are most attractive. Now, why the Florida highway department decided to stop demolition of the old Route 90 bridge after taking down half left me wondering if a county line didn't run down the middle of the river. Sort of tough bananas if an unsuspecting motorist was to take a wrong turn heading west down the old Route 90 on a dark and stormy night.

Old Rt. 90 Bridge

Cattahoochee River Dam

Looking the other way, upstream, one could see the Chattahoochee Dam, which was built to form Lake Seminole. This is the lake easily visible on the map at the beginning of this day's log. It looked like many small towns and farms were displaced by the lake water when this dam was built.

Acres of Tomatoes

It's quite possible I was still in too much pain to notice, but John passed acre after acre of tomato fields, remarking on how much dull work it must have been to pound in all the tomato stakes and how much dull work remained to be done tying up all the tomato branches. All tomatoes where I live are gown in greenhouses, and it never occurred to me that they might be grown commercially outdoors.

Bubba routed us north of Tallahassee on residential roads turning first right and then left, then up hills and down hills, and stopping at many four-way intersections. *(Don't forget to unclip your pedals, Sam)*. I finally arrived at the Tallahassee Best Western Hotel by mid afternoon having negotiated what John counted to be twenty-one turns to get there. Curiously enough, it appeared there were two Best Western's in Tallahassee, both were located right off Route 90 and both were across the street from a Denny's restaurant. The year before, during the 2014 C2C, Bubba had made reservations at one of them for his 2014 C2C. At that time he hadn't realized there were two and, as he approached Tallahassee in his Pampered Pedalers RV to check up on how well the Wolfpack was organizing the registration of incoming 2014 cyclists, he Googled the phone number for the wrong Best Western. Naturally he was told by the receptionist there was no reservation under his name and no cyclists anywhere around. When he asked if this was the one on Rt. 90 across from Denny's, the receptionist confirmed that it was. In a panic he called his Wolfpack captain and was informed that all was in order and all baggage had been placed in the correct hotel rooms. Of course Bubba then called the first Best Western back to ask what was up and got the same "Huh?" response. This went back and forth a few times before it finally penetrated that there might be two Best Westerns in Tallahassee. Bubba had us all in stitches during his daily after-dinner presentation as he told us about this misadventure.

Before dinner in the parking lot, I cornered Murph, our surrogate mechanic, bought one of his Continental Gator tires, and talked him into mounting it for me. These tires are the best money can buy, but they are extremely hard to mount as, being tough as they are, they don't stretch around the rims easily. I was grateful for Murph's extensive knowledge as he mounted the tire with relative ease.

Many of us used the Best Western laundry facility to do some clothes washing. Much as the free laundry service provided by the SAG team was appreciated, I found it was far easier to do it myself than have to paw through piles of look-alike clothing washed by the SAG team.

The night was oh-so-sweet as I nestled into my comfy motel bed.

Murph At Work

Roadside pickup today was a **Child's Rubber Ball that Lit Up from Inside When Thrown.**

April 23 - Day 48

Tallahassee to Madison
48 Miles

Map data ©2015 Google

Riding across the Florida panhandle these past few days had been some of the most relaxing riding I'd ever done in my life. The roads all had shoulders, the weather was warm and sunny, and the scenery was pastoral. The first SAG stop along our route was in the town of Monticello, named after Jefferson's home in Virginia. At one time, Monticello was a cotton growing center, and at another time it supplied eighty percent of all watermelon seeds in the US. Tupelo's Bakery was famous (in the area) for its cinnamon buns, so I ordered one and sat outside in the balmy morning air discussing with other Coasters how wonderful our ride in Florida had been up to then. I had this habit of comparing places we had passed through with the New Hampshire town in which I live, and few offered me any incentive to move except this small town of Monticello. It was an absolutely charming locale in a part of the country where it doesn't snow. For me that's a big draw.

Don Relaxing at Tupelos

Once we got past how great the weather and the ride was, our discussions meandered off into the future of riderless cars and how Don lost his leg. Don spent his professional career in the U.S. Coast Guard and then in the merchant marine, a career from which he retired all in one piece. Once retired, he decided he needed to clean the gutters on his house, a task during which he fell off his ladder and landed on a ceramic garden gnome. The fall shattered the bone in his leg so badly that his doctors recommended its removal and replacement with a prosthesis. It's amazing what they have accomplished with prosthetic designs these days, because if one didn't know that Don had lost his lower leg to amputation, one would never know anything had ever happened to him. The fact that he came with us on this 3,000 mile venture and completed it in style was such a wonderful inspiration. Don had also had another adventure he told us about later, an adventure involving a terrorist attack on a cargo ship on which he was serving as captain off Somalia. Stay tuned!

Our next SAG stop was in Greenville at the Haffye Hays Park known primarily for its bronze statue of the "Father of Soul," Ray Charles. Ray grew up in Greenville. His childhood home was just down the street from the park and is currently a museum, rebuilt from vine covered ruins only a few years ago. Ray grew up dirt poor in a segregated neighborhood where the homes had no indoor plumbing, no running water, and no electricity. Later on in Madison,

we heard a talk by one of his childhood friends, Virginia Prichard, who told us all the kids who played with him just accepted the fact he was going blind and made the best of it. Ray took piano lessons from Wiley Pitman, owner of the Red Wing Cafe, for a while when he could still see, but the lessons stopped when he turned totally blind at the age of seven. At this time, his mother sent him to a state-sponsored school, The Florida School for the Deaf and Blind in St. Augustine, where he again studied piano and learned to write music in braille. The deep sadness expressed in his music might have been due to his witnessing the

Ray Charles - Father of Soul

drowning of his younger brother when he still had his sight, a sadness that was surely deepened when he was fifteen and his mother died. While experimenting with many different musical genres, he eventually came up with his own, which the world now knows as "Soul."

Madison County Courthouse

Madison was our stop for the night at the campus of North Florida Community College. This was another lovely town with origins dating back to the early 1800s when cotton was king. The world's largest cotton gin was established in Madison before the boll weevil wiped out the industry in 1916. The courthouse was another spectacular example of European architecture, and it was beginning to look as if the same architectural firm had a stranglehold on southern courthouse design. They all more-or-less looked the same.

FLORIDA

Before stopping at the college gym where the Wolfpack would have had our duffle all set out and our air mattresses blown up, Tom and I met Linda in town and we did some sightseeing. I got a kick out of a sheriff's truck with a sign reading *"PURCHASED WITH CONFISCATED DRUG MONEY"* painted on its tailgate. The picture below shows Linda pointing to the sign. Our next stop was the town park celebrating the history of Madison. The flywheel driving the world's largest cotton gin was mounted for all to see, as well as a statue celebrating Roosevelt's four freedoms:

- Freedom of Speech
- Freedom of Religion
- Freedom from Want
- Freedom from Fear

Freedom from "want" wasn't one I had heard before, and was certainly one that needed further definition. In my experience the human capacity for "want" is bottomless, for as soon as most of us get what we think we want, we find we want something else. Since Roosevelt served during the depression, I imagine his definition of "want" probably stopped after food, shelter, clothing, and a job. It is interesting, though, that he recognized freedom from fear as being important. Buddha recognized the importance of this freedom 2500 years earlier, and he considered it the most important one.

Purchased With Drug Money

After our meanderings through the town of Madison, we stopped for a vanilla milk shake that contained three scoops of ice cream, a teaspoon of vanilla, and a splash of milk. Clearly I'll have to change my eating habits once the trip is over if I am to retain my rock hard abdominals honed to perfection by riding across America. *Ha!* When we finally returned to the college campus, we heard that Bill, the member of the 2014 C2C who dropped out to be with his wife after her traffic accident, had suffered from tachycardia earlier in the day and was in the college hospital emergency room. Bill recovered but was unable to rejoin the tour, which was sad because in the few days we had gotten to know Bill, he had become a valued addition to the group. He was sorely missed and we all wished him well.

The high point of the evening was a talk given by an amazing lady Bubba had met at the Haffye Hays Park in Greenville, the Virginia Pritchard mentioned above. She told us of the childhood she spent with her friend, Ray, and the games they used to play with him never fully realizing the difficulty he faced being blind. He was different, he coped, and all his young friends coped with him. When she then told us about her own life, I could do nothing but sit there, my mouth open, in rapt attention. She too had grown up in a house much like Ray's with no running water or electricity. She dropped out of high school when she became pregnant as a teen, then married, bore five children, and, when most of her peers had settled into a life of motherhood and penury, she decided to go back to school. Going back to school meant getting up before five am, catching one Greyhound bus and then another one to get her to school. She first finished her GED, then she attended Florida A&M to get her BS in Elementary Education. Her two older sons took care of cooking for the family, while a sitter came in for her youngest baby. All the schools she attended until her third year in college were segregated. She eventually graduated with a Master of Science degree in Elementary Education when she was thirty-five and then taught for thirty-eight years in Greenville. She ran for mayor of the town, was elected and held the position for fourteen years. As mayor, she was instrumental in the

Mayor Virginia Pritchard

reconstruction of Ray Charles' home and its establishment as a museum. She is currently Vice Mayor of Greenville. Hers was a success story that had me shaking my head in wonderment. What a lady. What a grand lady!

Roadside pickup for the day was a **Xmas stocking**

April 24 - Day 49

Madison to High Point Springs
77 Miles

Map data ©2015 Google

This day was the best day of the entire cross-country trip according to my blog, and as I review my blog entries while writing this book, I am aware that most days in the South

Just One Beautiful Ride

with warm, dry weather, and wide flat roads were the "best." Clearly, all the pain and suffering on chipseal, mountainous climbs, and narrow western back roads hadn't hardened me at all. Warm and fuzzy still won out over cold and prickly. Bubba could take a lot of credit for this, as he chose back roads for his Coasters with very low traffic, smooth pavement, and scenery that was all lush green fields or live oak forests. The picture on the previous page was one John took typical of many roads we traveled on this day. Pretty nice, eh?

Peanut Processing Plant

The first lush green field I passed was full of peanuts. I found that out as I stopped to take a picture of an enormous silo installation and garage for what must have been fifty semi-trailers. As I pulled into the driveway to take the shot, a manager let me know, laughing, that I'd made a wrong turn. He then went on to tell me that most of the fields in the area contained peanuts, and the ones at his installation were all used for peanut butter. And I thought Georgia had a corner on peanuts!

You Sure You Got That Spelled Right?

From there, I crossed over the Suwannee River made famous by Stephen Foster's song. I kept looking at the spelling and looking at the spelling, just absolutely sure I'd been taught the spelling was "Swanee" not "Suwannee." When I asked Gail, one of the retired elementary school teachers on the tour, she confirmed my impression that the correct spelling was "Swanee." Sure enough, it did appear that ol'

Stevie spelled it "Swanee" as Gail and I consulted everyone's now dubious source for straight skinny in the age of the internet, Wikipedia, and there it was confirmed that Stephen Foster spelled it "Swanee." However, the people of Florida have spelled it "Suwannee" since time immemorial and Google Maps also spells the river "Suwannee," so Steve was misled. We should cut him some slack, though, as he had never even seen the river itself when he wrote the song. We ran into some pretty hysterical misspellings on signs further along, so stay tuned. The scene I photographed looking down river from the bridge crossing the Suwannee was lovely.

Bubba suggested we stop for lunch at Bob Butts BBQ. It was only eleven o'clock when I got there, so I didn't sample any of his fare. But, as usual, my mind started to wander as I pedaled away, and I wondered if the "butts" were beef buttocks or pork buttocks. Then, *no it couldn't be*, was Bob's last name really Butts? Once I got there, I began to imagine the kind of hazing he took as a child for having a name like Butts. I had never run into the name Butts before, so I felt if it was his last name, it must have been a name foreshortened at some time during his forefathers' immigrant past. Pursuing this line of reasoning, I learned, again from our great source for the straight skinny, that the

Way Down Upon

name Butt had its origins in French. *But* in french means goal or target and was a name given to archers or those who lived close to archery ranges. William the Conqueror granted lands in Middlesex, England to William de Butte who is listed in the year 1200 as an owner of lands in Orseney. I am now satisfied Bob had French DNA in his blood, and he could have defended his name with pride against childhood taunts. Thank you Wikipedia, you're forgiven.

Hind Quarters for Lunch?

We were staying at the O'Leno State Park just outside High Springs, and, as I entered the park, I was cautioned to be wary of gophers on the road. At first blush I, an arrogant Yankee, had to laugh heartily at the ignorance of the Floridian sign painter who didn't know the difference between a gopher and a turtle. My own ignorance was pointed out to me when I was informed that "Gopher Tortoise" is a term given to a specific kind of tortoise that lives in florida. They're a threatened species, and I needed no encouragement to stop wherever I was on my bike to help them across the roads. Then again, you already knew that.

Our residence at the park included a number of cabins arranged in a semi-circle around a community center. The Santa Fe River runs right through the park behind the community center. There was a trail down the side of the river to a sink hole where the river dropped underground for three miles before it reappeared on the surface again. We walked down to the sinkhole and watched as a huge whirlpool slowly circled around the entrance. There was an alligator sitting on a log in the green algae accumulated on the surface. You can barely make him out in the photo.

Santa Fe River Sinkhole

The next day was a rest day and some of us Coasters would be heading out to rent canoes and kayaks and drift down the same Sante Fe River that was disappearing into the sink hole shown above. We would be starting our drift after the river reappears from its three mile subterranean passage. I got to wondering if any SCUBA divers had followed the river through its underground passage. I can't imagine anyone daring enough to try such a stunt, but then spelunking is right up there with rattlesnakes on my list of earthly terrors.

Roadside pickup today was a **Pair of Sunglasses**

April 25 - Day 50

High Point Springs
Rest Day

Sam and John Photo Op

After breakfast, those of us who chose to paddle down the Santa Fe River headed out to the canoe rental agency in vans provided by the agency. John Holden and I rented one together and hammed it up for a photo op prior to our departure. The river itself was a most interesting study, as it starts in the swamps of the North and joins the Suwannee many miles down stream. The swamps generate a murky detritus that turns the upper Santa Fe into an opaque, acid tea. As this tea moves south it encounters sandstone and limestone which suck it into the ground, filter out the opaque, and deliver it as clear spring water in the lower Santa Fe. As we paddled down the river, we could see the springs bubbling up from inside the banks and churning to the surface.

Crusin' Along Singin' a Song

Gophers? They Are Now!

We also saw many, many turtles (gophers?) sunning themselves on logs in the river. Can you see them well enough in the picture to count them? John counted thirteen but I only found twelve. How many can you find?

One of the more interesting sidelights along the river was the home of Naked Bob, whose shanty stood at the source of Lily Spring, a spring that wells up twenty million gallons of water a day. From his home Bob gives passersby advice on how to live their lives. You can just make out Bob and his shack beyond the end of the canoe where he is sitting behind a partition in deference to the easily embarrassed. He had a captive audience when we stopped, so we thought it best to slip away without hearing his spin on the world. There were plenty of signs posted around, broadcasting his views on peace, love, and minimalist living. John and I had heard that once he gets going it is hard to get him to stop.

Naked Bob and Lily Spring

The banks of the Santa Fe were lined with cyprus trees whose roots dug deep into the soil under the river. We were told that there was little oxygen where their roots lay, so they needed to send up shoots, which absorbed oxygen from the air. These shoots looked like stalagmites popping up all around the bases of the full grown trees. They were almost gnome-like in their statuesque presence along the river banks, and could easily be mistaken for new trees taking root.

At the end of a relaxing day in the canoe, John and I pulled up on the bank and waited for the van to take us back to O'Leno Park, where a presentation by Captain Don Grosse awaited us. Don was the amazing fellow with the prosthetic leg mentioned earlier, and his presentation was about a sea faring adventure he had, following his career in the US Coast Guard. After retiring from the USGC, he continued his love of the sea as a merchant marine captain, and was unfortunate enough to captain the Liberty Sun when it was attacked by pirates off the coast of Somalia.

Cyprus Roots Breathing Air

Captain Don was well aware of the pirate menace, and had attached every high pressure water hose his ship carried along the sides of the vessel in order to thwart any attempt by pirates to scale the side of the ship. Sure enough, there the pirates came and sure enough, Captain Don ordered the hoses turned on. He then sent his entire crew down to the engine room for safety while he rode out the attack. Apparently, the pirates were well-acquainted with the layout of the ship's quarters, and one of their objectives in this raid was to kill the captain in order to deny the crew their leader. In carrying out this objective, they shot a rocket-propelled grenade into Don's stateroom a few minutes after he had gone to the bridge. The grenade completely destroyed his stateroom and would have killed him had he stayed behind a minute longer. Because the water cannons prevented the pirates from boarding the Liberty Sun, they satisfied their frustration by peppering the superstructure with automatic rifle fire before eventually departing.

The Liberty Sun was attacked the same day that the Maersk Alabama was attacked, when Captain Phillips was taken hostage. I had heard of the Maersk Alabama attack and had seen the movie starring Tom Hanks as Captain Phillips, but I had no idea there was another ship undergoing a similar attack at the same time. Don told us that once American flag ships were under siege from pirates, Congress quickly passed legislation allowing the merchant fleet to bear arms. Subsequently, the attacks stopped. Duh! Don then let on that another reason the attacks stopped was the mysterious explosive destruction of all the pirate mother ships along the Somali coastline. Was it the work of Navy Seals? Who knows? Actually we all thought Don knew, but when queried, he simply smiled and asked for the next question. His accounting of this experience held us all transfixed. What a guy!

While many of us were paddling down the Santa Fe River, Linda and company were fashioning a Roadside Virgin out of the bits and pieces of roadside detritus picked up since the beginning of the trip. The bag of stuff covered two fold-up tables, and selecting what to use and what to discard became a major undertaking. Linda had created many Virgin of Guadalupe icons in the past, and she had a pretty good idea what she was going to use. The life jacket served as the body of the Virgin, the old shoes as her feet, and the gloves as the rays of light emitted from her pure soul. Linda explained that even virgins have a dark side, so the pornographic DVD was attached to her back. As soon as dinner was cleared, I brought the virgin in, covered in a black plastic bag and set on a table in front of the group. The idea was that Linda would be introduced, come in, uncover the virgin, and present it to Bubba.

In the end there was just so much road junk to use, Linda decided to use some for the Virgin, and some as a costume she would wear to present the Virgin. She would become the Bicycle Bag Lady of Bubba's C2C. So when I gave her the cue, in Linda sashayed wearing the red wig, the sunglasses, and the Vince Camuto shoes. In fact, everything you see Linda wearing in her picture on the next page we Coasters picked up alongside the route of our travels. The group loved it with hoots and hollers and much laughter. Linda then removed the black plastic covering and there she stood, the statue of the 2015 C2C Virgin of Guadalupe, made entirely from roadside castoffs save maybe the face cut from a magazine. The mission of this Virgin was to protect Bubba and all his Pampered Pedalers on future rides wherever they may go. Bubba had tears in his eyes as he accepted his gift.

High Point Springs was certainly a high point of our trip.

Roadside Virgin and Bicycle Bag Lady

April 26 - Day 51

High Springs to Palatka
85 Miles

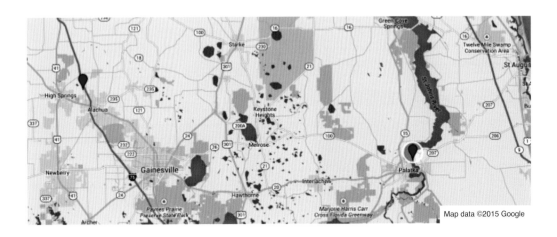

Map data ©2015 Google

Those of us anticipating rain and making suitable preparations in our habit weren't disappointed on this day, our fifty-first on the road. We got it all: heat, humidity, thunder, lightning, and torrential cloudbursts. As a result, the opportunity for taking pictures was curtailed, but given better weather I might have taken a shot of an "Historic Gainesville" sign. What it did was get me wondering what makes a town "historic." It seemed every other town we went through in the South welcomed us to its historic past, but then every past is historic, isn't it? The internet definition of historic is, "famous or important in history, or potentially so." How famous does a town have to be to be called

Hawthorne Bike Path

"famous?" Who gets to write the history, anyway? And, "potentially"? How does that fit in? Come to think of it I'm historic according to this definition. I'm sure this book has the potential to sell millions of copies and then I'll become famous and qualify for the title of historic. Actually my grandchildren consider me historic, but it's not because they think I'm famous or important in history. They consider me historic because I'm old.

Our route circumnavigated Gainesville and included a bike path that took us through the woods, far from the madding traffic, to Hawthorne. It rained hard, but rain wasn't as nerve wracking to me when biking as was lightning. The fact that nobody really knows for sure where it will strike next made it all the more nerve wracking, because there isn't one best answer for what to do. We are advised not to stand under a tree. OK, no trees, but maybe the bolt of lightning thinks my bike is a tree. When I ride in a thunderstorm I feel like I'm on a surfboard with sharks swimming all around just waiting to attack me. While riding on this lovely bike path with Linda, there was a horrendously loud *CRACK* that seemed to land right next to us. They say, internet again, a person's chance of getting struck by lightning in one's lifetime is about 1 in 12,000, but that statistic is based on the world population and the total number of lightning strikes hitting the planet in an average lifetime. I have a feeling the odds go way, way up while riding a bike under a thundercloud.

Hey Waiter

The sun finally did come out and along with it so did my camera. I just had to stop and photograph a couple of signs I saw as we entered Hawthorne. Mr. Business' business had gone out of business, perhaps because of what we might consider an unwise choice of nomenclature for his enterprise. "Hey waiter, there's a hair in my Mu Gu Gai Pan."

A little further on, we were treated to advertising for a car repair shop, the owner of which might have used the same consultant for his enterprise as did Mr. Business. It's hard for me to understand any small businessman who wouldn't make the effort to at least get the spelling right in his advertising. But then I'm a Yankee and don't make any pretense about understanding Southern attitudes. Both these businesses sure got my attention and maybe that was the idea.

Excuse Me?

After a simply gorgeous afternoon Tom, Linda, and I pulled into Palatka, where we immediately hit the Dairy Queen. Several nights before we were given a presentation by the head of a bicycle group in Florida, a group that had successfully lobbied for a paved bike trail across the state linking the West coast to the East coast. We all felt

Palatka Dairy Queen

a DQ every twenty-five miles would be an appropriate goal for which to lobby as well. I had two root beer floats at this stop; I was wondering if you would ask.

Palatka is another "historic" town with links to the railroad. Murals decorated town buildings testifying to its history, the one across from the DQ being focused on this link was one of the most colorful.

Toot, Toot

Then there was an "historic" Episcopal Church across from the DQ. The architecture of this structure was particularly appealing, made more so by the spanish moss hanging from the live oak trees in its yard. An eighty-five year-old man running a crab shack across the street felt the church was at least a hundred years old as it had been there his whole life.

Historic Episcopal Church

The Florida National Guard served as our host for the night at their local armory. Bubba had us all gather after dinner for a humorous exercise when he went through every town in which we had stayed and asked each of us in turn what we remembered about the trip that day. It was comical how I could have spent so much time riding through the country, but couldn't put together the events in my memory with the name of a town. I was asked about Gila Bend, and my mind went blank. I could remember absolutely nothing about it except it was named after a bend in the Gila river. Do you remember anything about Gila Bend? Doesn't really stick in your mind, does it? I wish Bubba had asked me about Tombstone - now there was a town I remembered in exquisite detail.

Before ending our gathering, Graham, who was from England, related an hysterical account of the morning he went stumbling into the men's room, eyes barely open, to brush his teeth. He thought the toothpaste tasted funny, and when he looked at the tube he discovered he had been brushing his teeth with the "Butt Butter" we all use to anoint our crotches prior to a ride. In the midst of hoots and laughter someone, probably Eddy, blurted out, "Where did you put your toothpaste?" to more hoots and laughter. It was a bitter-sweet last evening, as we were brought face-to-face with the realization the trip would be over in just one more day. The following day we'd be pulling into St. Augustine, the end of our journey. It had been an amazing adventure, and most of us were sad it was coming to an end. We had formed some fast friendships that will endure to the end of our lives. Hopefully we would see each other again on future Bubba treks.

April 27 - Day 52

Palatka to St. Augustine
44 MILES

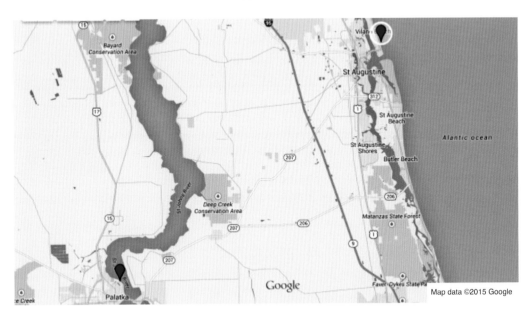

Map data ©2015 Google

We Coasters had a short ride this last day, only forty-four miles, but the route took us down back roads that totally changed my impression of Florida. Once one leaves the cities, Florida is a beautiful state populated with warm, friendly people. It's also populated with many interesting sights. Take, for instance, the Rust Museum, home to hundreds of rusted out pieces of once useful farm equipment. There were hulks of tractors, plows, harrows, seeders, and many other farm implements I couldn't identify that filled acres with their rusted remains. This seeder in the photo is just one example of the many mothballed implements. Actually, I'm not sure if it was a museum proper, probably just a junkyard, but still fascinating to stop and ponder.

The Rust Museum

The route passed more roadside memorials, but these seemed to be state sponsored, as the signs were all the same. Maybe the families had to buy them from the state. Each was individually decorated often with some indication of what interested the deceased. Clifford Johnson seemed to have had an interest in boxing, note the gloves hanging below the wreath in the picture to the right.

Bye Cliff

As I stopped to take a picture of this memorial, a kindly middle aged, obviously very poor black man stopped to chat. He asked me a number of questions about the cross country trek, and then he asked me where I called "home." When I said "New Hampshire," he immediately lit up with recognition and said, "Oh, the state capital is Concord, isn't it?" I was stunned for a minute, because there are probably people in New Hampshire who don't know Concord is the capital, and here a poor southern black knew instantly. Sometime in his past, he must have studied state capitols and New Hampshire had stayed with him. I congratulated him, shook his hand, and wished him well in his life journey - maybe a hollow wish, but a heartfelt wish nonetheless.

City Hall

And then I pulled into St. Augustine, originally a Spanish city established in 1565 and reputedly the oldest city in America. The historic (old?) section was without question one of the most beautifully restored of any I had ever visited. The town offices were magnificent, as were the buildings of Flagler College and the Flagler Hotel, all built in a renaissance Spanish style by Henry Flagler, a railroad tycoon and one of the richest people in the world at the time. The place was a tourist mecca,

and I wish I had had more time to hang out and appreciate its beauty.

As I tooled into town, I could hear cheers and whistles as earlier arrivals greeted me from the balcony of the A1A Ale Works. The cheers and whistles got louder as each newcomer added his or her voice to the cacophony. It was quite a spectacle, and one the many tourists milling about seemed to appreciate. Little by little, we all finished lunch and slowly

Lunch at the A1A

made our way across the Intercostal Waterway to a McDonald's, where we were scheduled to rendezvous for a group photo before our final run to the beach.

Group Shot Prior to Our Final Parade to the Ocean

Our destination for the night was the Hampton Inn on St. Augustine Beach. After the group photo in front of the beach welcome sign, we all formed a single file and headed the mile or so down the beachfront road. Don Grosse was chosen to lead the group, as his perseverance in pursuing an active lifestyle following the injury to his leg provided such inspiration to us all. As we paraded down the beach front road, we cut a mean swath with our matching Coast-to-Coast jerseys. Cars honked, onlookers clapped, and restaurant patrons cheered us to our final destination from open balconies. It was a tremendously emotional parade of forty very, very proud riders having accomplished a goal few in America would even consider setting for themselves at any age.

Upon reaching the Hampton Inn, we went right through the lobby out to the beach where we all dipped our front wheels into the Atlantic Ocean. Many riders had family and friends come to congratulate them on their success, and the beach scene was a pandaemonium of people all hugging, giving each other high fives, and posing for photographs. We had done it. We had planned for a year, worked hard to get into shape, and actually ridden our bicycles across America. What an accomplishment!

Wheel Dipping in the Atlantic

The grand finale was a celebratory dinner after which Bubba presented each rider with a medallion commemorating the trip together with a framed photo of each rider at some point along the way. We often saw Ed Gillette, our spiritual leader, sitting by the side of the road taking pictures as we rode past, and what a remarkable effort it was for him to get the pictures all developed and mounted in a frame so they could be presented to us at the end of the trip. Thank you Ed!

This Coast-to-Coast bicycle trip across America was unquestionably a most rewarding adventure, and I know all us Coasters will cherish the memories we have of it forever.

Aging Well

2015 Coaster Joe Nelson

Aging well is not just well aged
For that there are things that are perfectly staged
There is cheese, scotch, and remarkable wine
Special ingredients, handling and timing that's fine

Aging well has ingredients and handling that's true
What's unique about your product is the handler is you
At first takes a life, well lived or perhaps not
Some with work and careers, some stay at home with a tot

Our lives seem as natural as a squirrel up a tree
We are all a bit unique in how we decide to be
It is the same with this aging so well
What is special to us is like the DNA in a cell

Given this process that is our singular choice
There are ways we can enhance this beautiful voice
Yoga, TaiChi, and meditation so calm
Bring spiritual connection from the mind to the palm

Improving health, wellness and quality of life
Well practiced they reduce inflammation and lower your strife
These actions influence our mind, body, soul
And encourage the aged to be aged whole

Some have health that starts to fail and deteriorate
Others choose to retire, watch TV, for death they just wait
Most don't think this is aging so well
They actually think this is a living hell

Some instead run marathons to eighty five
Living intentionally in the moment to keep them alive
It is in this energetic way we come to age well
With acceptance and courage we cast our own spell

Others decide to bike with Bubba from coast to coast
These ones are determined to make life the most
This group bikes mountains and deserts, from C2C
Because living life fully is the way they choose to be